true FRIENDSHIP

How to ... Study series

Series Editor:
TERRY VIRGO

true FRIENDSHIP

DUNCAN WATKINSON

WORD BOOKS
Nelson WORD LTD
Milton Keynes, England
WORD AUSTRALIA
Kilsyth, Australia
WORD COMMUNICATIONS LTD
Vancouver, B.C., Canada
STRUIK CHRISTIAN BOOKS (PTY) LTD
Cape Town, South Africa
JOINT DISTRIBUTORS SINGAPORE -
ALBY COMMERCIAL ENTERPRISES PTE LTD
and
CAMPUS CRUSADE, ASIA LTD
PHILIPPINE CAMPUS CRUSADE FOR CHRIST
Quezon City, Philippines
CHRISTIAN MARKETING NEW ZEALAND LTD
Havelock North, New Zealand
JENSCO LTD
Hong Kong
SALVATION BOOK CENTRE
Malaysia

TRUE FRIENDSHIP

ISBN 0-85009-657-X (Australia 1-86258-340-4)

Created, designed and typeset by Frontier Publishing International Ltd., BN43 6RE, England. Reproduced, printed and bound in Great Britain for Nelson Word Ltd. by Cox and Wyman Ltd., Reading.

94 95 96 97 / 10 9 8 7 6 5 4 3 2 1

A Friendly Word

When I first mentioned to my wife, Vasanti, that I was thinking of writing a book about friendship, she laughed. She had every reason to — she's the one who makes friends easily while I tend to be shy and 'cool'. She's often 'the life and soul of the party' while I struggle to be even mildly friendly. But as I reflected on this, I realised that it is precisely because I'm not 'naturally' a friendly person that it might be appropriate for me to write this book.

The Lord has spent many years teaching me even the basics of friendship. I know that I've learned something because I have two very good friends in Bombay — Arun Philip and David Fernandes — who are the best friends I've ever had. Their friendship has been a great strength and encouragement to me over the past twelve years.

This book owes much to Vasanti, Arun and David and reflects what they are as well as what they've taught me. Another friend, Ranjit Rodrigues, has brought together sermons I've preached and material I've produced to help bring this book about.

The material is probably best studied with somebody else — preferably someone you want to know as a friend. But it will also help you if you study it alone. Vasanti and I have worked through most of the material with our three 'children' (aged 11–17) and have found that it stimulated us as a family and gave us many topics for open discussion and prayer.

My hope is that this book will help both naturally friendly and unfriendly people to develop and enjoy deeper friendships with others.

Duncan Watkinson

Also available in the *How To* series:

Battle for the Mind	David Holden
Being Sure of the Bible	Arnold Bell
Effective Evangelism	Ben Davies
Enjoying God's Grace	Terry Virgo
Facing Life's Problems	Frank Gamble
Growing Up as a Christian	Roger Day
Handling Your Money	John Houghton
Honouring Marriage	John and Liz Wilthew
Joining the Church	Richard Haydon-Knowell
Knowing God's Will	Phil Rogers
Leading a Housegroup	Richard Haydon-Knowell
Learning to Worship	Phil Rogers
Praying the Lord's Prayer	Terry Virgo
Presenting Jesus in the Open Air	Mike Sprenger
Receiving the Holy Spirit and His Gifts	Terry Virgo and Phil Rogers
Seeking the Kingdom	John Hosier
Working for God	Ralph Turner

Foreword

The *How To* series has been published with a definite purpose in view. It provides a set of workbooks suitable either for housegroups or individuals who want to study a particular Bible theme in a practical way. The goal is not simply to look up verses and fill up pages of a notebook, but to fill in gaps in our lives and so increase our fruitfulness and our knowledge of God.

Both of Peter's letters were written to 'stimulate ... wholesome thinking' (2 Pet. 3:1). He required his readers to think as well as read! We hope the training manual approach of this book will have the same effect. Stop, think, apply and act are key words.

If you are using the book on your own, we suggest you work through the chapters systematically, Bible and notebook at your side and pen in hand. If you are doing it as a group activity, it is probably best to do all the initial reading and task work before the group sessions — this gives more time for discussion on key issues which may be raised.

Unless otherwise stated, all quotations from the Bible are from the New International Version.

Terry Virgo
Series Editor

Contents

Chapter One

Introducing Friendship

> All the lonely people, where do they all come from?
> All the lonely people, where do they all belong?[1]

These lines from 'Eleanor Rigby', a 1966 Beatles song, capture the widespread loneliness in the world today. It's a sad fact that more and more people have fewer and fewer real friends. A recent survey in America suggested that under 10 per cent of American men have a genuine friend. Yet after God had created Adam, He declared:

> It is not good for the man to be alone (Gen. 2:18).

This principle is especially true for marriage, which is why God then created Eve, but it is also true in life. We are social beings, not isolated individuals. We were created with a need for friends and a desire to enjoy healthy, warm, lasting relationships with others. Yet, we see that genuine friendships are uncommon and often fail to last very long.

I became aware of my own weakness in forming genuine friendships when I realised to my shame that I'm not in contact with anyone from school or college days, or from those I knew at work before I came to India in 1981. In those days, 'Friends' were just people who happened to be around — I didn't give much, and I didn't receive much either. I know that I'm sadly typical of many and I'm also aware that there are millions who've experienced even less real friendship than I have.

Consider as many reasons as you can for the loneliness and lack of friendship in the world.

If you are doing this study with others, why not take turns in sharing your thoughts. One way of deepening your friendships is to be more open about your ideas — so here's an opportunity to start!

If you are studying this book on your own, I strongly urge you to write down your thoughts in a notebook before moving on to the next section.

THE REAL REASON

All the points you have considered will probably contribute to the problem, but the Bible takes us to the root cause, which is perhaps deeper than we may realise. All our reasons are really just symptoms of sin. When Adam was created, he enjoyed a relationship with God. The Lord spoke with him, provided for him, considered his feelings and cared for him. God brought Eve into this healthy relationship and the scene was set for them to enjoy being together.

Sadly, these friendships — with God and one another — did not last because Adam disobeyed His Creator. He ate the fruit from the one tree that was forbidden to him and incurred spiritual death (Gen. 2:17) and exclusion from the Garden of Eden (Gen. 3:23). The Bible calls Adam's disobedience 'sin'.

Read Romans 5:12 and answer the following questions:

How did sin enter the world?
What came as the result of sin?
Who does death come to?
Why does death come?

As head of the human race, Adam passed his separation from God to all mankind. Everyone is sinful and is cut off from God because of sin. Since we all fall short of God's glory (Rom. 3:23), none of us can live up to what God expects us to be. This also means that we are enemies of God.

> the sinful mind is hostile to God (Rom. 8:7).

Because sin always results in isolation and alienation, Adam's sin not only separated him from God, but soon led to broken relationships between people. After Adam was banished from the Garden, there was conflict between his two sons, Cain and Abel. (Gen. 4:1–12). When Cain asked God, 'Am I my brother's keeper?' (Gen. 4:9), he revealed that he no longer felt any sense of concern or responsibility for his brother. His lack of concern brought about the first murder in history.

Sin separates people from God and from one another. Alienation from God has resulted in a world which is steeped in sin and doesn't know right from wrong. Alienation from others has led to divorce, rejected children, suicide, apartheid, violence, war and loneliness. History has shown that these problems cannot be solved by legislation, official decrees or increased niceness to others.

RECONCILIATION

All mankind is in this terrible mess, separated from God and unable to maintain healthy friendships. People are in a totally hopeless situation which they are powerless to change. Thankfully God has intervened as Paul tells us:

> Once you were alienated from God and were enemies in your minds because of your evil behaviour. But now he has reconciled you by Christ's physical body through death (Col. 1:21,22).

It's important to know two things. First and foremost this reconciliation is an act of God. People of every religion try to find some way to work themselves back into a relationship with Him — and they all fail. There is nothing we can do to get ourselves right with Him and to remove the pain of separation. Secondly, it is the physical death of Jesus on the Cross which has made this reconciliation possible. Jesus' work on the cross is summarised in 2 Corinthians 5:19.

> Read this verse and note the two things God was doing.

God knew that we were alienated from Him and grieved over our sin. His love for us was so great that He decided to pay the world's costliest price by sending His Son to die for us and to reconcile us to Himself.

One dictionary definition of 'reconcile' is 'to make friendly after estrangement'. The death of Jesus revealed that God wants us to be His friends. It took away the barrier of sin so that we could be brought back into a relationship with God.

Adam's sin caused breakdown in relationships, but Christ's death brings their restoration. Those who put their faith in Christ are the most privileged people on earth! They have been reconciled to God and are now in a position to start enjoying healthy relationships with others.

FRIENDSHIP — THE PRACTICE OF JESUS

When Jesus came to earth, He was a 'friend of sinners'. As His followers, we are called to imitate His life of friendship. One reason the Pharisees could not accept Jesus as God centred on the company He kept. He was continually eating with 'tax collectors and sinners' (Luke 5:30). Of His twelve close friends, one was an ex-tax collector, some were fishermen and one was a thief! Yet when He chose them, He wasn't just recruiting a group of men to carry on His work after His departure.

> Look up John 15:15.
>
> What does Jesus call His disciples now?
>
> Read Matthew 26:50.
>
> How did He address His betrayer?

Jesus went about being a friend and making friends. As head of the Church, He wants friendship to be an important part of church life too.

FRIENDSHIP — A GOAL OF THE CHURCH

The reconciliation of the Cross is not just a spiritual reality which sorts things out between God and individuals. God expects it to be visibly expressed as we come together to enjoy our relationship with Him and with one another. Friendships are the fabric of the church, although church history has not always given a very good demonstration of this. God's people should never serve through 'religious' or 'arms-length' relationships, but with genuine friendship.

> Read Acts 2:46,47 and note how the early church practised friendship.

The early church had neither buildings nor New Testament, but they did have one another. Friendship was a hallmark of the early church. They enjoyed following the Lord together and they helped, strengthened and encouraged each other. Even Josephus, a secular historian of that day, noticed this and wrote, 'See how these Christians love one another!'

CONCLUSION

If you do not yet know God as a friend, you can be reconciled to Him now if you:

Recognise that sin is a barrier between you and Him.
Believe that Jesus Christ died to remove this barrier by paying the penalty for your sins on the Cross.
Ask God to forgive you all your sins so that you can be reconciled to Him.
Make a commitment to God to turn away from your sinful ways and to live a life of obedience to Him.
Thank Him for hearing you and for giving you eternal life.

If you already know God as a friend, consider some of the ways in which He has demonstrated that friendship.

Later we will see that God wants us to act in similar ways towards our friends. Our understanding of friendship comes from Him, so before finishing this lesson why don't you spend a little time thanking God for all that He has done in His friendship with you.

---

[1] 'Eleanor Rigby', words and music by John Lennon and Paul McCartney.

Chapter Two

FRIENDSHIP AND FRIENDLINESS

Real friendships are possible because of the Cross. Yet the word 'friend' means a variety of things. Sometimes we use it to describe a person who is simply friendly — he says 'Hi!' when you pass him in the street. Sometimes a friend is someone who shares every detail of our life and continues to love us regardless of what we may say or do.

We need to distinguish between 'friendliness' and genuine friendship. Friendliness is an important starting point towards friendship and we need to cultivate it with everybody we meet. It does not have great depth, but it has warmth and helps to create an atmosphere in which friendships can develop. There is, however, a danger in failing to go beyond friendliness.

Read Proverbs 18:24.

Who is the person who may come to ruin? How do you think he (or she!) may come to ruin even though (s)he has so many companions? Who sticks closer than a brother?

Having 'many companions' is not wrong in itself, but it may hinder our developing deep friendships. Some people excel at superficial relationships and gather facts and information about a wide circle of acquaintances. But for various reasons they are never able to form quality friendships. 'Companions' — casual acquaintances — are not the same as real friends.

We should of course be friendly to everyone, but we should be aiming to have friends at many deeper levels too. At the 'top' end of the 'friendship' scale, there should be a few people with whom we enjoy deep, intimate and warm friendship which is characterised by complete openness and honesty. Between the casual and deep relationships there will be a range of different friendships which can be described on a graph.

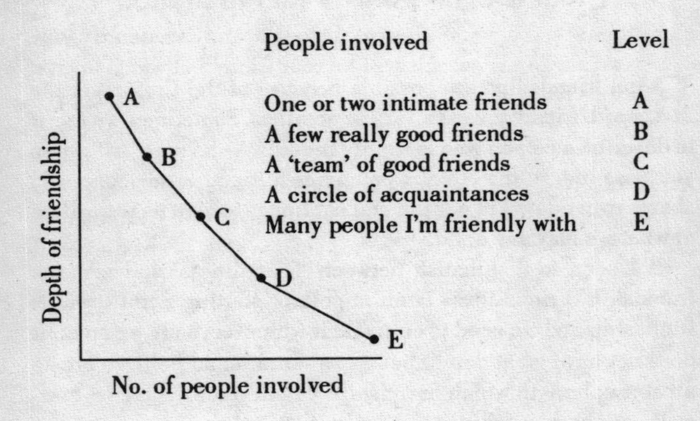

People involved	Level
One or two intimate friends	A
A few really good friends	B
A 'team' of good friends	C
A circle of acquaintances	D
Many people I'm friendly with	E

Sad to say, there is a Level F somewhere off the graph. It describes the person who is totally friendless — uninvolved with anyone at any depth. We will look at each of these levels of friendship and see how Jesus functioned at each of them.

LEVEL F

As I've just said, people at level F have no friends, not even casual acquaintances. Thousands of years ago, David felt this way.

> Look to my right and see; no-one is concerned for me. I have no refuge; no-one cares for my life (Ps. 142:4).

You've probably faced times like these — in fact you may be going through such a time right now. You may even have felt like giving up on everything. As we said, the Lord Jesus is our model of friendship and even He was totally abandoned by His friends — as Isaiah explains:

> **He was despised and rejected by men; a man of sorrows and familiar with suffering (Isa. 53:3).**

Jesus knew what it was like to be left alone and can identify with you if you are friendless. He will be your friend but wants to give you friends too.

LEVEL E

At this broadest level, Jesus had a great number of followers — the gospels tell us that crowds of people pursued Him. Although we don't know the level of these friendships, He always seemed willing to give some time to anybody who came to Him.

> Read Matthew 19:13,14 and Mark 10:46–52.
>
> Note the people to whom Jesus responded warmly. Do you think He knew these people before?

LEVEL D

Jesus had a large group of disciples whom He must have known on a slightly deeper level than those in the crowds. We can assume that they spent time with Him and that He taught and trained them to some degree.

> Read Luke 10:1 and note the number of disciples that Jesus appointed here.

LEVEL C

> Read Mark 3:13.
>
> On what basis did Jesus decide to gather a more intimate group of twelve disciples?

This verse indicates that Jesus wanted these men to be His friends for His sake as well as theirs. He wanted to have a circle of friends who were closer to Him than the larger group.

LEVEL B

There were special occasions when Jesus selected an inner group of only three of the Twelve. This was presumably because He felt close to them and wanted to share more of Himself with them.

> Whom did Jesus take with Him in Mark 5:37; 9:2; and 14:33?

LEVEL A

Even within this trio there was one disciple who was more convinced of Jesus' love than the others.

> Read John 13:23 and note how John describes this closest friend.

This person is mentioned in the same way in John 21:20 and most commentators agree that his name is John. There was a special rapport between Jesus and John. Perhaps that was one reason why the other disciples were so angry when John's mother wanted special favours for her boys! (Matt. 20:20ff) When Jesus was on the Cross He demonstrated His special relationship with 'the disciple whom he loved' by asking him to look after Mary, His mother (John 19:26,27).

I believe that Jesus wants us to follow His example by operating at all these levels of friendship. It surprises me how low people's expectation of friendship really is. Somebody who from my point of view is at Level C, may describe me as his best friend. That's because he doesn't realise that the relationship can possibly be deeper. Although I'm flattered, I'm also sad that he isn't closer to somebody else. One purpose of this book is to encourage you to raise your sights in terms of friendships.

Naturally, it's impossible to have all your friendships at Level A. But it is possible to be friendly towards everyone. A normal Christian doesn't delight in distance but in closeness. However, it's sad to hear Christians complaining that they have no friends, which is all too often true. John Wesley often quoted some advice that he received from an elderly Lincolnshire clergyman:

> The Bible knows nothing of solitary religion. Sir, you wish to serve God and go to heaven? Remember, you cannot serve God alone. You must therefore find companions or make them.

The best way of getting friends is to be a friend, and the best starting point is to be friendly to everyone. Friendliness is the seed bed in which friendships start to grow and develop. For most of us this requires deliberate effort. We must learn to:

BE RESPECTFUL AND COURTEOUS

People today often live private, withdrawn lives — an Englishman's home is his castle. It almost seems wrong to intrude or interfere in another's life, so we end up being indifferent. Some branches of Hinduism actually teach that it's wrong to get involved with somebody in need, because you are interfering with their 'karma' or destiny.

Plain old-fashioned respect is disappearing as neighbours pass each other without so much as a nod. In fact, the courtroom is one of the few places where people rise in respect. Peter says:

> Show proper respect to everyone (1 Pet. 2:17).

Respect simply means putting a high value on others. This shows them that you regard them as valuable. It may mean standing up when they come into the room, holding a door open to let them go through first, or letting somebody go ahead of you in the queue. All of these actions, and many others, show that you value an individual.

GREET WARMLY

First impressions count! We demonstrate how approachable we are by the way we greet others. Are we cheerful and encouraging, or are we for ever caught up in our own thoughts and oblivious to everybody else?

When I was at boarding school, we had to greet teachers and students in authority with a glance at their faces and a clear 'Good morning, sir!' It was a good discipline and is a minimum for those who want to grow in friendship.

Read Matthew 5:47.

Is there anything special about greeting your brothers?

Here are a few tips on greeting people:

Be the first to speak.
Look them in the eye.
Be enthusiastic and warm.
Use first names as far as possible.
Introduce yourself clearly and personally as appropriate.
Go beyond the superficial 'Hi!' and 'Have a nice day'.

CONVERSE

Many of us really do need to develop the art of conversation. I come across people who have few friends and when I try talking to them, I can understand why. They simply have no 'small talk.' Not every conversation is going to be profoundly theological and we need to be able to chat about everyday matters: the weather, the price of eggs, the latest sporting results, etc. This sort of talk is a way of being friendly.

A great way to express friendliness is to ask questions. I have an aunt who used to be an interviewer on the BBC. It doesn't matter who you are, whenever you talk to her the conversation is always interesting. The reason is that she has learned how to ask questions which get people talking, and to show genuine interest in the answers. We may not reach her standard, but we can certainly work at asking questions.

When you encounter someone for the first time, what sort of questions could you ask which might lead into deeper conversation?

Questions are a great way of starting conversations, but we should also be ready to talk about ourselves and share about our own lives. If we only ask questions, it will seem more like a police interrogation than an attempt to be friendly.

BE HELPFUL

Here is another area where Christians should distinguish themselves from unbelievers. The biblical idea of friendly fellowship is most apparent when members of God's family share time, money, possessions and life with each other. Luke gives us a glimpse into the life of the early church:

> All the believers were one in heart and mind. No-one claimed that any of his possessions was his own, but they shared everything they had (Acts 4:32).

No wonder they enjoyed the favour of the people! They were helpful people to have as neighbours. I'm sure you can think of many ways in which you could help people. It's a good start to be willing to help at the time of need, but it's even better if you learn to be sensitive so that you can anticipate the help which will be required.

BE AVAILABLE

You'll never be a friendly person unless you give time to it. If your life is clogged up with all sorts of other things, you won't feel like being friendly to the man in the corner shop or to that person opposite you on the train. God wants us to be friendly, and we must give time to it.

Read Proverbs 17:17.

When should a friend show love?

Rate your availability to be a friend on the following scale by circling the most appropriate number (0 = not at all; 10 = always).

0 1 2 3 4 5 6 7 8 9 10

Obviously Jesus wants us to be aiming for a 10. If that's what you've scored I'd love to meet you! If you've scored anything less than 10, you will know that there is room for improvement. You might find it helpful to write down some specific practical steps you can take to help you to become more friendly.

Chapter Three

Benefits of Friendship

Growing as a friend requires effort, and it's easy to think, 'Is it worth the trouble?' I'm sure many of 'the lonely people' gave up on friendship because they were hurt or rejected when they tried to be friends. Even for Christians, friendship does not come automatically.

In his book, *Strengthening Your Grip*, Charles Swindoll said,

> ... we are like a pack of porcupines on a frigid wintry night. The cold drives us closer together into a tight huddle to keep warm. As we begin to snuggle really close, our sharp quills cause us to jab and prick each other — a condition which forces us apart. But before long we start getting cold, so we move back to get warm again, only to stab and puncture each other once more. And so we participate in this strange, rhythmic "tribal dance". We cannot deny it, we need each other, yet we needle each other![1]

> To dwell above with saints we love,
> That will be grace and glory.
> To live below with saints we know;
> That's another story![2]

Solomon was given a wise and discerning heart (1 Kings 3:12) and wrote about the importance of friendship. In Ecclesiastes 4:9–12 he gives four reasons why 'two are better than one'.

Read Ecclesiastes 4:9–12.

FRUITFULNESS

Two are better than one, because they have a good return for their work (Eccl. 4:9).

This verse speaks about fruitfulness and effectiveness. Two friends can achieve far more, and in a more satisfying way, than someone on his own. This may be why Jesus sent His disciples out 'two by two' (Luke 10:1). It was probably each pair, rather than individuals, who 'returned with joy and said, "Lord, even the demons submit to us in your name"' (Luke 10:17). Similarly, the first recorded miracle in Acts features the healing of a cripple by two disciples, Peter and John (Acts 3:1–8).

Consider occasions when you and a friend have been able to accomplish things more enjoyably and productively because you have been together.

HELPFULNESS

If one falls down, his friend can help him up. But pity the man who falls and has no-one to help him up! (Eccl. 4:10)

Here the emphasis is on help. A friend is there when you need him.

The book of Ruth demonstrates how one individual can give a new lease of life to another. Naomi was very bitter because the Lord had brought her so much misfortune. Her husband and sons had died and she'd been left in a foreign land. She urged her two daughters-in-law to go back to their families while she returned to Bethlehem, but Ruth insisted on staying with her. Ruth's friendship and help restored Naomi and brought the blessing of God on her family.

Think of a time in your life when you were struggling and somebody came along and helped you.

WARMTH

Also, if two lie down together, they will keep warm. But how can one keep warm alone? (Eccl. 4:11)

This is a picture of warmth, companionship and mutual encouragement. When Paul and Silas were in Philippi, they must have been glad of each other's company when they were arrested, flogged, thrown into the inner cell of a prison and put in the stocks (Acts 16:24). Would they have been so keen to pray and sing hymns to God on their own? Maybe. But it was bound to be much easier when they were together.

We will be devoting a chapter to encouragement later in the book, but right now, think of a time when a friend's encouragement helped you through.

PROTECTION

Though one may be overpowered, two can defend themselves (Eccl. 4:12).

Friendship protects us physically, emotionally and spiritually. David and Jonathan enjoyed tremendous friendship and one of its hallmarks was Jonathan's willingness to protect David from his father, Saul.

In 1 Samuel 19:2, Jonathan warned David that Saul was 'looking for a chance to kill you.' On this occasion, he was able to persuade Saul not to harm David. Later, he risked his life to protect David from Saul. Not only did Jonathan protect David, he strengthened him emotionally — through his warm expressions of love — and spiritually — by drawing him closer to God.

This protection is not only against others who might want to harm me, it can also be a defence against myself. Sometimes I get worked up over a situation and start planning some rash action. It's then that I'm grateful for a friend who comes alongside and says something like, 'Now, Duncan, you know that's not really going to help ...' Such words stop me from acting in an ungodly way.

Recall when a friend has protected you in this way.

THE KEY TO FRIENDSHIP

A cord of three strands is not quickly broken (Eccl. 4:12).

Having talked about 'twos', Solomon suddenly slips into a 'three'. This reminds us that God must stand at the heart of every friendship. He's the third cord and will not allow friendships which exclude Him to prosper. If two people keep Him out of their relationship, He may permit problems which turn the friendship sour, or allow differences to develop which we are unable to resolve without Him.

Consider how you can keep Jesus at the centre of a relationship with someone who is not a Christian.

We must remember that our goal is primarily to please God, not to make friends. But having said that, God still wants me to have friends and to use my friendships to serve His purposes.

SUMMARY

God's plan for friendship lies in the four benefits Solomon mentions: Fruitfulness, Helpfulness, Warmth and Protection. He wants you to be this sort of friend, to enjoy this sort of friendship and to keep Jesus at the centre of your life

Pray now that the Lord will:
Make you a genuine friend.
Give you genuine friends.

HOW FRIENDLY AM I REALLY?

The test below has been devised to help you look at yourself in each of the four areas in Ecclesiastes 4:9–12. To make it more specific, I have put a number of adjectives under each heading. You should assess yourself somewhere along each line, e.g. if you tend to get angry quickly and fail to show self-control, your score will be about '3'. If you are self-controlled and only occasionally get angry, then your score will be a '7' or '8'.

Circle the number that best describes you in each of the following areas:

A. FRUITFULNESS

1. Angry 0 1 2 3 4 5 6 7 8 9 10 Self-controlled

2. Impatient 0 1 2 3 4 5 6 7 8 9 10 Patient

3. Independent 0 1 2 3 4 5 6 7 8 9 10 God-dependent

4. Disloyal 0 1 2 3 4 5 6 7 8 9 10 Loyal

5. Dominating 0 1 2 3 4 5 6 7 8 9 10 Submissive

B. HELPFULNESS

1. Self-conscious 0 1 2 3 4 5 6 7 8 9 10 Free

2. Grumbling 0 1 2 3 4 5 6 7 8 9 10 Thankful

3. Selfish	0	1	2	3	4	5	6	7	8	9	10	Considerate
4. Insensitive	0	1	2	3	4	5	6	7	8	9	10	Alert
5. Suspicious	0	1	2	3	4	5	6	7	8	9	10	Trusting

C. WARMTH

1. Harsh	0	1	2	3	4	5	6	7	8	9	10	Merciful
2. Envying	0	1	2	3	4	5	6	7	8	9	10	Appreciative
3. Boastful	0	1	2	3	4	5	6	7	8	9	10	Modest
4. Critical	0	1	2	3	4	5	6	7	8	9	10	Encouraging
5. Hypocritical	0	1	2	3	4	5	6	7	8	9	10	Real

D. PROTECTION

1. Competitive	0	1	2	3	4	5	6	7	8	9	10	Uncompetitive
2. Quarrelsome	0	1	2	3	4	5	6	7	8	9	10	Peaceful
3. Defensive	0	1	2	3	4	5	6	7	8	9	10	Correctable
4. Unteachable	0	1	2	3	4	5	6	7	8	9	10	Teachable
5. Resentful	0	1	2	3	4	5	6	7	8	9	10	Forgiving

The value in this questionnaire lies in noting the areas in which you feel strong and weak. Once you've completed it, I suggest that you take two of your weaker points and ask the Lord to help you change in them. Then look out for divine opportunities to behave differently — they're sure to come!

You may also find it worthwhile to give a blank copy of this form to a close friend or relative and ask them to score you. If you do this, be aware that the person who is assessing you may have a different standard from you, e.g. his idea of patience may seem very different from yours. Instead, you must look for the relatively high and low scores. Then you can thank God for the former and get working on the latter!

---

[1] *Strengthening Your Grip* by Charles Swindoll © 1983 by Charles R Swindoll. Hodder & Stoughton Ltd./USA, Philippines & Canada, Word Publishing, Dallas, Texas. All rights reserved.

[2] *Great Church Fights* by Leslie Flynn. Published by Victor Books © 1976 SP Publications Inc., Wheaton, IL 60187.

Chapter Four

Barriers to Friendship

Some of us really want to be good friends with others, but find that things keep going wrong. King Saul knew something of this because he didn't appear to have many friends. He seemed to make a mess of his relationships, and found difficulty trusting anyone. He argued with his son, Jonathan, and tried to kill him. And he was continually opposed to David despite David's kindness and loyalty to him. As a lonely old man, he made a desperate, evil attempt to recall Samuel from the dead, and ended his life in tragic suicide. Yet Saul was a man who had met powerfully with God:

> Has not the LORD anointed you leader over his inheritance? (1 Sam. 10:1)
>
> God changed Saul's heart (1 Sam. 10:9).
>
> the Spirit of God came upon him in power and he joined in their prophesying (1 Sam. 10:10).

Saul was a charismatic figure with a genuine conversion experience and a bright future ahead. Yet in spite of these things, everything went wrong and ended in tragedy. One reason for this was that he didn't have strong relationships with others. At times of pressure and loneliness he had no genuine, caring friends to whom he could turn.

The biblical account of Saul's life suggests that he had a number of barriers to friendship — things that prevented him from relating well to others. I hope that as you read about these barriers,

God will help you to pinpoint any similar barriers in your life, give you grace to deal with them and enable you to enjoy friendships as He intended.

SELF-SUFFICIENCY

Read 1 Samuel 13:7–14.

Saul was in a tight spot, up against a tough enemy with his own troops deserting him. He was new to the whole business of ruling and the prophet Samuel, who had promised to come, had failed to arrive.

Note how Saul's fear prompted him to react (v. 12).

This is something that comes naturally to many of us — taking matters into our own hands and trying to manage affairs without involving God or others. We like to be in charge so we refuse to humble ourselves and ask for help. Yet God is the only person who has all the necessary resources to be self-sufficient.

When man fell into sin, he destroyed His relationship with God and was forced to be self-sufficient, depending on his own natural abilities. In this sense Man became 'like God' as Satan had promised Eve (Gen. 3:5). But God never designed man for independence, as Jesus underlines:

> If a man remains in me and I in him, he will bear much fruit; apart from me you can do nothing (John 15:5).

'Nothing' is very difficult for a self-sufficient person to accept! When we have too much confidence in our own abilities, we will think, 'I can make it alone'. Actually, without God, we wouldn't even be able to breathe! I find it hard not to be self-sufficient because I was a 'manager' before I became a Christian. I've had to learn to repent whenever God convicts me of an arrogant independence.

Self-sufficiency is often manifested in our attitude to our friends. Paul taught the Corinthians how to depend on, value and respond to each other.

Read about this in 1 Corinthians 12:12–27.

Paul cherished this sort of friendship, as the ending of most of his letters reveals. A remarkable practical demonstration of his love for an individual is found in 2 Corinthians 2:12,13.

Read these verses and note why Paul refused to stay in Troas.

How dependent are you on your friends? Rate yourself on this scale by circling the most appropriate number (0 = Absolutely independent; 10 = Totally dependent).

0 1 2 3 4 5 6 7 8 9 10

Consider some ways in which you show your friends that you depend on them.

SELF-REJECTION

Before he became king, Saul was described as:

> an impressive young man without equal among the Israelites — a head taller than any of the others (1 Sam. 9:2).

He looked good, but clearly struggled to accept himself as he was. We know this because at the time he was to be proclaimed king, he hid among the baggage (1 Sam. 10:20–23).

Think of some reasons why he did this.

Have you ever felt like 'hiding among the baggage'? I know I have. Maybe I'm walking into a crowded room, or attending a conference where everybody else seems to know each other. On these occasions, the baggage somehow seems much more attractive! All too easily we disqualify ourselves from the love of friends by rejecting ourselves in the first place.

According to Romans 15:7, how are we told to accept one another?

Remind yourself of four things that were wrong with you when Christ accepted you.

Since Christ has accepted me just as I am, I don't need to set standards for myself that are higher than His. His Word tells me that:

> I am fearfully and wonderfully made (Ps. 139:14).

and that:

> All the days ordained for me were written in your book before one of them came to be (Ps. 139:16).

This means that God oversees every detail about you, your life and circumstances. He likes you just as you are, not as you think you ought to be. The Bible says:

> he will rejoice over you with singing (Zeph. 3:17).

If you're unsure about God's total acceptance of you, then you will always be vulnerable to self-rejection. This will in turn hinder you as you seek to establish genuine, lasting friendships.

Check if any of the following have ever stopped you from developing friendships:
Lack of money, physical appearance, clothes, past failures, job, others' opinions of you, educational background, speech/accent, family, spouse.

Take time now to talk honestly to God about any of these (or other) areas where you have been disqualifying yourself.

Thank Him that He really accepts you just as you are, 'warts and all'.

Ask Him to remind you of His unconditional acceptance as you engage in deeper friendships.

Don't think that everybody else is focusing on that little 'wart' of yours — most of the time they don't even notice it!

SELF-PITY

Saul's difficulty in accepting himself spiralled him into self-pity. He rejected himself and reacted with the attitude 'poor me!'

> Read 1 Samuel 22:8 and note the three accusations that Saul levelled against his officials.

How sad it is that the valiant commander of Israel should descend so low as to start making petty accusations against his own subordinates! Self-pity makes us so preoccupied with our own hardships that we have little capacity for making and developing quality relationships. It drags us into a downward spiral where no one can really draw close to us, because 'nobody understands'.

Self-pity feeds on suspicion. Saul thought that his own men were siding against him and that he was all alone. Suspicion kills friendship because it forever questions the other's motives, words and actions. 'What did he really mean when he said ... ?' 'He's only visiting me because ...' Christian love calls us to assume the best about a person and to trust him.

> Read 1 Corinthians 13:7 and note the four things that love always does.

The next verse tells us that love 'never fails'. Christians must overcome self-pity and suspicion, and let their lives overflow with God's kind of love.

If you've been wallowing in self-pity, ask God to forgive you now, and resolve not to succumb to it again. Ask Him to help you show His love as you develop friendships with others

Ask God to help you to manifest His love as you develop friendships with others.

APPROVAL-SEEKING

Saul's insecurity made him struggle to win the approval of people.

> Read 1 Samuel 15:24–31.
>
> Note the reason that Saul gave for his disobedience (v. 24). Note also his concern for his image before the people (v. 30).

Saul was more worried about what people thought of him, than about God's reaction to him. We can easily fall into the same trap by being wrongly concerned about our appearance and what people will think of our actions. We can even do godly things, e.g. aiming for excellence, giving generously but be motivated by the hope that others will notice and approve of us.

Here are some indicators of approval seeking. Make a note of any which you've noticed yourself doing.

Expecting thanks for things you do for others.
Feeling the need to 'keep up' with your friends when it comes to spending.
Being disappointed if your friends don't comment on your new clothes or hairstyle.
Talking about your achievements when you're getting to know people.
Behaving differently when you know you're being watched.

We need to know that God approves of us; His approval is nowhere clearer than in the cross. He values us so highly that He was willing to send His Son to die for us. When we realise how great His love is for us, we will stop struggling to win the acclaim of others and seek only to please Him.

COMPARISON

Saul was also friendless because he constantly compared his achievements with the successes of others.

Read 1 Samuel 18:5–9. What upset Saul?

What do you think is actually meant by 'a jealous eye?'

The relationship between Saul and David began to break down at the point where Saul could not cope with David's success. David was 'better' than him.

There will always be people who are better than us — better looking, better equipped, better dressed, better educated or sometimes, just better off! The world tells us that 'comparisons are odious,' but more than that, they can kill friendship. I need to know that I have been uniquely crafted by God and that I am the best person at being me!

We reveal whether we are free of the sin of comparison by asking ourselves, 'Do I genuinely rejoice in the successes of others?'

Ask yourself this question and reply honestly to it. If you know that you struggle in this, ask God to help you.
Praise God for three people whose gifts seem to excel over yours. Pray God's richest blessing on them.
Cultivate the habit of appreciating others to their face. This may be hard at first, but will become easier and it will open the doors to deeper friendships.

FEAR

In spite of his kingly role, Saul was a very fearful man. We've already seen that he was afraid of the people (1 Sam. 15:24). But he was also 'dismayed and terrified' of Goliath (1 Sam. 17:11), and when he saw the Philistine army, 'terror filled his heart' (1 Sam. 28:5).

Fear can dominate our lives and prevent us from making and enjoying friendships, prompting us to ask the following kinds of questions:

What if I say the wrong thing?
What if they find out about that part of my life?
What if we have a disagreement?
What if they knew what I'm really like?
What if they just ignore me?

Consider the effects on your friendships if you think in this way.

I have to overcome fear by choosing not to let it control me and by reminding myself that God's perfect love for me drives out fear (1 John 4:18). I cannot stop the thoughts and emotions coming, but I can choose to reach out in friendship despite what I feel inside. This is part of the principle which Paul talks about when he says:

> Do not be overcome by evil, but overcome evil with good (Rom. 12:21).

Poor Saul died friendless, but there's no reason why we should. God wants us to break through the barriers of self-sufficiency, self-rejection, self-pity, approval-seeking, comparison and fear. His grace is sufficient. Let's appropriate it.

Chapter Five

ONE ANOTHER

'And they'll know we are Christians by our love,'[1] the song declares with faith and a little optimism. In a world of sad and lonely people, God is building His radiant church — a community of individuals who are learning not be individualistic. The New Testament Church certainly seemed to catch this vision and live it out convincingly.

Read Acts 2:42–47; 4:32–35 and 6:1–4.

Consider the atmosphere in the Jerusalem church.

LOVING FRIENDSHIPS

There is only one basis for all friendships — love. The apostle John always preached on love. It is said that when he was so old that he couldn't walk, he was carried out on a stretcher to the waiting crowds. He had just one message: 'love one another' (1 John 3:11). When asked why he didn't say anything else, he apparently replied, 'If you do that, you've done all.'

Read 1 Peter 1:22 and note the kind of love that Christians should have for their brothers.

Here, Peter is not telling his hearers to work at getting this kind of love. He is assuming that since they are born again, they already have it.

The word 'sincere' comes from two Latin words meaning 'without wax'. In early days it was sometimes used with reference to bell-making. When molten metal was poured into a bell cast, it often contained airholes. These looked unsightly, so the holes would be filled up with wax to make the casting appear perfect. The trouble was that although the bell looked good, it would sound muffled. A 'sincere' casting contained no wax and the bell sounded clear and true.

In Chapter One we saw the danger of 'religious' and 'arms-length' relationships. God wants us to enjoy friendships that are sincere and from the heart.

Read Romans 12:9, 10 and note the biblical standard of love.

QUALITIES OF LOVE

Since love is so vital in Christian friendship, we will look at it in more detail.

IT IS UNCONDITIONAL

God loves us completely. He demonstrated His love by sending Jesus to die for us while we were still opposed to him. He wants us to imitate His love (John 15:12).

Someone once described true Christian friendship as 'abandoning one's right to quit'. Friendship must be for ever — not on fire one week and forgotten the next. Perhaps you've experienced or seen friendships which have tended to come and go.

Why do you think this happens?

IT IS SACRIFICIAL

Christian love is about laying down your life. A woman once asked her husband, 'Would you be willing to die for me?' After careful thought, he replied, 'My love for you is an undying love!' It was a brilliant answer, but neither God's intention nor Jesus' example.

Read John 15:12,13.

What is the greatest demonstration of love?

Not all of us will be asked to die physically for our friends. But we can all lay down our lives in other ways — through our minds (what we think), wills (what we want) and emotions (what we feel). How would you answer these three questions?:

If your friend denies doing what you strongly think he did, would you be willing to give him/her the benefit of the doubt?

If your friend wants to go to a different place for the picnic you are planning together, would you be willing to go where he/she wants to go?

If your friend has upset you, are you willing to forgive him/her and put the matter behind you?

IT IS ALWAYS DEPENDABLE

God sets His standard for dependability when he tells us:

> Never will I leave you; never will I forsake you (Heb. 13:5).

'Just call and I'll be there' should be a distinguishing mark of Christian friendships. We must learn to be available and dependable. The Bible doesn't tell us to love others at convenient times, but at 'all times' (Prov. 17:17).

IT IS ACTION-BASED

Christian love isn't some vague, sentimental feeling. John says:

> Dear children, let us not love with words or tongue but with actions and in truth (1 John 3:18).

And James declares:

> What good is it, my brothers, if a man claims to have faith but has no deeds? (James 2:14)

Love is something you do. It's expressed in practical acts of kindness which range from hospitality and visiting, to odd jobs. Friendships can't be made in meetings. A congregation that cannot enjoy a picnic together cannot truly break bread together.

Virtually every book in the New Testament tells us how God wants us to demonstrate our love. We would benefit from a study of the verses which include the phrase 'one another' or 'each other'. They fall into four main areas: Acceptance, Service, Relating positively, Handling differences.

ONE ANOTHERING

Read and note what the following verses say about 'one another' friendship. Then evaluate yourself on a scale of 0 to 10 (0 = Never; 10 = Always).

ACCEPTANCE

Romans 15:7	Accept others as they are	____
Romans 16:16	Greet warmly with enthusiasm	____
Ephesians 4:32	Am kind and compassionate	____

SERVICE

Romans 12:10	Honour others above myself	____
Galatians 5:13	Serve in love	____
Ephesians 5:21	Submit	____
1 Peter 4:9	Offer hospitality	____
1 Peter 5:5	Clothe myself with humility	____

RELATING POSITIVELY

Ephesians 5:19	Speak godly words	____
1 Thessalonians 5:11	Encourage	____

Hebrews 10:24	Spur others on	____

HANDLING DIFFERENCES

Romans 12:16	Live in harmony with others	____
Romans 14:13	Do not judge (condemn)	____
Ephesians 4:2	Am forbearing	____
Colossians 3:13	Forgive	____
Colossians 3:16	Teach and admonish	____
James 4:11	Avoid slander	____
	Total	____

At the end of this chapter you'll find a similar list to give to a friend to assess you. Give him/her the freedom to be totally honest! The feedback should help you. You will also find a list for group use.

Spend time now:
Thanking God for the areas in which you feel you are doing well.
Asking Him to help you to grow in your weak areas to make you a better friend.

ONE ANOTHERING

A friend's assessment

Ask your friend to read through the following list of 'one anothers' and to evaluate you according to what he/she thinks (0 = Never; 10 = Always).

ACCEPTANCE

Romans 15:7	Accepts others as they are	____
Romans 16:16	Greets warmly with enthusiasm	____
Ephesians 4:32	Is kind and compassionate	____

SERVICE

Romans 12:10	Honours others above self	____
Galatians 5:13	Serves in love	____
Ephesians 5:21	Submits	____
1 Peter 4:9	Offers hospitality	____
1 Peter 5:5	Clothes self with humility	____

RELATING POSITIVELY

Ephesians 5:19	Speaks godly words	____
1 Thessalonians 5:11	Encourages	____
Hebrews 10:24	Spurs others on	____

HANDLING DIFFERENCES

Romans 12:16	Lives in harmony with others	____
Romans 14:13	Does not judge (condemn)	____
Ephesians 4:2	Is forbearing	____
Colossians 3:13	Forgives	____
Colossians 3:16	Teaches and admonishes	____
James 4:11	Avoids slander	____
	Total	____

ONE ANOTHERING

GROUP ASSESSMENT

The attached list contains several Bible instructions on 'one-anothering'. Each member can write down the names/initials of each of the others at the top of the page, rate each one (0 = Never; 10 = Always) in the four categories and total the scores at the end of each category. The focus should be on the relatively higher and lower scores, rather than on the absolute values.

Once each member has added up the totals for each of the other members in the group, the individual totals for each category should be combined and the average worked out. For example, if there are 8 people in the group and their combined score for Tony under 'Acceptance' is 62, then the mark given to Tony should be 62 divided by 8 which is 7.8.

It might be an idea to appoint one mathematically gifted person in the group to do all the sums for everybody and to bring the results back the next time you meet.

Fill in the name of each person in the group and rate out of 10.

ACCEPTANCE

Rom. 15:7	☐	☐	☐	☐	☐	☐	☐	☐	☐	☐	☐	Accepts others
Rom. 16:16	☐	☐	☐	☐	☐	☐	☐	☐	☐	☐	☐	Greets warmly
Eph. 4:32	☐	☐	☐	☐	☐	☐	☐	☐	☐	☐	☐	Kind/ compassionate
Total	☐	☐	☐	☐	☐	☐	☐	☐	☐	☐	☐	

SERVICE

Rom. 12:10	☐	☐	☐	☐	☐	☐	☐	☐	☐	☐	☐	Honours others above self
Gal. 5:13	☐	☐	☐	☐	☐	☐	☐	☐	☐	☐	☐	Serves in love
Eph. 5:21	☐	☐	☐	☐	☐	☐	☐	☐	☐	☐	☐	Submits
1 Pet. 4:9	☐	☐	☐	☐	☐	☐	☐	☐	☐	☐	☐	Hospitable
1 Pet. 5:5	☐	☐	☐	☐	☐	☐	☐	☐	☐	☐	☐	Humble
Total	☐	☐	☐	☐	☐	☐	☐	☐	☐	☐	☐	

RELATING POSITIVELY

Eph. 5:19	❑❑❑❑❑❑❑❑❑❑❑❑❑❑	Speaks godly words
1 Thess. 5:11	❑❑❑❑❑❑❑❑❑❑❑❑❑❑	Encourages
Heb. 10:24	❑❑❑❑❑❑❑❑❑❑❑❑❑❑	Spurs others on
Total	❑❑❑❑❑❑❑❑❑❑❑❑❑❑	

HANDLING DIFFERENCES

Rom. 12:16	❑❑❑❑❑❑❑❑❑❑❑❑❑❑	Lives in harmony
Rom. 14:13	❑❑❑❑❑❑❑❑❑❑❑❑❑❑	Does not judge
Eph. 4:2	❑❑❑❑❑❑❑❑❑❑❑❑❑❑	Forbears
Col. 3:13	❑❑❑❑❑❑❑❑❑❑❑❑❑❑	Forgives
Col. 3:16	❑❑❑❑❑❑❑❑❑❑❑❑❑❑	Teaches/ admonishes
James 4:11	❑❑❑❑❑❑❑❑❑❑❑❑❑❑	Avoids slander
Total	❑❑❑❑❑❑❑❑❑❑❑❑❑❑	

---

[1] 'We are one in the Spirit' by Peter Scholtes. © Lorenz Corporation. Reproduced by kind permission of William Elkin Music Services.

Chapter Six

SERVANTHOOD

One quality which supports and strengthens all the Bible verses on 'one another' is servanthood — which is a fundamental characteristic of the life of Jesus. Service has never been popular — even among friends — but it is closely connected with friendship, as Jesus points out:

> **I no longer call you servants, because a servant does not know his master's business. Instead, I have called you friends (John 15:15).**

Service is at the heart of New Testament Christianity. Jesus' disciples 'graduated' to friendship through the training process of service. What was true for them will also be true for us.

> Read through the following verses and note the way in which the New Testament leaders described themselves:
>
> James 1:1
> Jude v. 1
> 2 Peter 1:1
> Romans 1:1

Paul was probably the busiest New Testament character of all. While he was writing a large chunk of the New Testament, he was also functioning as an apostle, travelling extensively, planting churches and appointing elders. But in spite of all this activity, he always remained a servant.

He wasn't working for God for what he could get out of it — he says himself that he never coveted anyone's possessions (Acts 20:32–35). Instead, he laboured with his own hands to supply not just his own needs, but also the needs of his companions. He worked hard at every task, diligently serving those who were weaker.

Read Acts 20:35.

Paul probably got his understanding of servanthood from the life of Jesus Himself. Jesus set the model — serving both God and man.

JESUS SERVED GOD

Jesus served His Father with all His heart, soul, mind and strength. At a time of terrible temptation, He firmly rebuked Satan, declaring:

> it is written: 'Worship the Lord your God, and serve him only' (Matt. 4:10).

A little later He taught the people that:

> No-one can serve two masters (Matt. 6:24).

And He declared:

> My food ... is to do the will of him who sent me and to finish his work (John 4:34).

Jesus' basic purpose in life was not to do His own thing, but to accomplish God's will. He therefore chose to ignore other distractions. We mustn't assume that it was easy for Him to do this, since we're told:

Although he was a son, he learned obedience from what he suffered (Heb. 5:8).

Jesus really wanted to serve God, and this meant that He obeyed His Father even when obedience was costly.

JESUS SERVED MEN

Jesus, the perfect servant, continually served others. Perhaps the greatest demonstration of His service is found in John 13:1–17.

Read it through carefully, trying to picture the scene as if you were there yourself.

If we look at the way Jesus served, we will see a number of common features. Service is:

COMPASSIONATE

Jesus wasn't just alert to God's requirements. He was also aware of the needs of people around Him. When He saw the crowds on the hillside, He felt compassion for them because they didn't have anything to eat (Mark 8:2). Again, He knew that when His disciples came to the Last Supper, their feet would be dusty and in need of a wash. Repeatedly we see Jesus' great sensitivity to people and His compassionate acts on their behalf.

DIRTY

When Jesus washed the disciples' feet, He was performing a task that was despised and usually left to the lowest of slaves. In a hot and dusty country like India, the feet are still regarded as the most 'undesirable' part of the body. If your foot accidentally touches a person, you are expected to apologise quickly and profusely.

Read John 13:1.

What did Jesus want to show His disciples?

On one occasion, Jesus healed a leper by reaching out and touching him. Lepers were considered untouchable in Jesus' day. They lived outside the city and warned passers-by not to approach by crying, 'Unclean, unclean!' wherever they went. Jesus was willing to 'get dirty' by making physical contact with him.

ORGANISED

Serving is often a spontaneous act, but it sometimes needs organising. Some of us never get into serving, because we're never ready for it. Jesus was!

> Read John 13:5 and note the three things that Jesus had ready so that He could serve His disciples.

SACRIFICIAL

Jesus had no 9–5 job! He was continually serving others. On occasions He was probably tired and dirty. He had His own 'problems' to think about too, but He always made an effort to demonstrate His love for others.

We read that Jesus received Nicodemus 'at night' (John 3:2). And when the crowds came to Him, He didn't hold back, but willingly taught them. Ultimately, He gave His life to serve mankind.

> Read Mark 10:45 aloud and slowly to yourself.

BLOCKS TO SERVING

None of us finds serving easy. If Jesus was tempted in every way just as we are, maybe even He had to overcome certain things when He knelt down and washed the disciples' feet. Let's look at some of the possibilities.

SELF-CONSCIOUSNESS

Many of us genuinely want to serve others but are too shy to do so. We feel surrounded by a shell of self-consciousness which keeps us stuck in our place. 'What will people think of me?' we question. 'Am I invading their privacy?' 'What happens if I muff it?'

These are all challenging questions, but they stem from a preoccupation with self, and not from an awareness of what God has done in our lives. Jesus was able to serve because He was secure. He was not living for people but for God.

> John 13:3 tells us three things that Jesus knew.
> What were they?

Jesus was able to wash feet because He knew His identity! His security didn't lie in what He did or didn't do, but in who He was. As God's Son, He could do all that God wanted Him to do, including washing feet!

If you're born again, you are also God's son and will one day be with Jesus for ever. If you know who you are in Christ, you'll push aside all the questions that hold you back in your service. Rather, you will be willing to do even the dirtiest of jobs regardless of what people think of you.

Recall an unpleasant job that you were asked to do recently.
It may have been at home, at work, at college or in the church.
Consider whether your reaction was appropriate.

INACTION

Once we refuse to succumb to shyness or self-consciousness, we must get on with serving. It would be absurd to get all prepared to serve and then do nothing!

> Read John 13:4,5 and note the six things that Jesus actually did.

Jesus wanted His disciples to see something behind His selfless actions. The washing of their feet was meant to be an example of service and love (v. 15). Once Jesus was seated at the table again, He said:

> **Now that you know these things, you will be blessed if you do them (John 13:17).**

DISTRACTIONS

As we get down to serving others, we will often meet distractions. When Jesus came to Peter's feet, His servant heart must have felt the pressure of Peter's objections and He would have been strongly tempted to stop serving. Even if you don't see jobs as 'beneath you', you will soon come across others who do!

> Why do you think Peter objected to Jesus' foot-washing activities? (John 13:8).

In spite of the protests, Jesus persisted in washing the feet of Peter and all the disciples. When we serve each other, we're doing God's will. Paul reminds us that whenever we do something for someone else:

> **It is the Lord Christ you are serving (Col. 3:24).**

PREJUDICE

We may wonder what Jesus was thinking when He came to Judas' feet. Judas had already arranged to betray Him, and Jesus knew it (John 13:11). How would you have coped with such a situation? I might have been tempted to make some excuse to miss him out and divert attention away from what was happening. Jesus served.

If we know that when we serve people we are serving Christ, then we won't worry about the identity of the person in front of us. Jesus washed the feet of those who would prove to be the most faithful to Him; He washed the feet of His betrayer.

Some of the people who come to my house are a joy to serve. I'd do anything for them. Sadly, I don't feel the same way about everyone who walks through my front door. In some cases, my natural inclination is to serve them as little as possible. The reason for this is prejudice. I've decided that some people are 'worthy' of being served and that others are not. That is unchristian.

Consider some of the people whom you would find it hard to serve, e.g. a difficult neighbour, people of other races, a work colleague, etc.

Ask God to help you serve everyone as Jesus did.

Chapter Seven

SELFISHNESS

We weren't born as servants — rather the opposite. Our natural state is selfish and most of us have been brought up in an environment which has encouraged us to remain that way. 'Look after No. 1', the world teaches. 'Don't let people take advantage of you! You've got rights, you know!' If we want to be serving friends, we must deal with the selfishness that has shaped the way we think and react. To help us overcome selfishness, we need to start by recognising it.

Work through the following questionnaire and score yourself as honestly as possible.

1 = Never
2 = Occasionally
3 = Every so often
4 = Sometimes
5 = Quite often
6 = Usually
7 = Always

When the doorbell rings, I wait for someone to answer it. ___
I'm annoyed when people don't greet me at church. ___
In conversation I frequently talk about my achievements. ___
I'm angry when someone keeps me waiting for an appointment. ___
When reporting on a disagreement, I avoid talking about things that put me in a bad light. ___
It takes some time for me to notice that someone is absent. ___

When someone is talking, my mind often wanders. ___
I avoid meeting certain people because I don't want to get involved. ___
I find it hard to speak words of love and appreciation. ___
I'm upset when somebody interrupts my plans for a relaxed evening at home. ___
I'm upset when somebody else gets the credit for what I've done. ___
When I enter a room, I'm conscious of people looking at me. ___
I forget to pass on messages. ___
I feel it's OK to keep someone waiting for me if I'm involved in something important. ___
I feel threatened when I'm corrected. ___
I continue reading the paper when others come into the room. ___
I only give lifts to those who are going where I am. ___
I leave the bill in the restaurant for others to pay. ___
I don't return things soon after borrowing them. ___
I wait for someone else to do a job that needs to be done. ___
I find it hard to pray for others. ___
I want to use the bathroom first, even if others are waiting. ___
I don't lend things for fear that they won't be returned. ___
I do other things while talking on the phone. ___
I find it difficult to be honest about my weaknesses. ___
Total ___

Hopefully this questionnaire will expose real life situations where you tend to behave selfishly — the higher you score against a comment, the more selfish you are in that situation! Your total score may amuse your friends, but its main goal is to help you to note the high score situations so that you can work at changing them.

Selfishness and servanthood are opposites. One grabs, the other gives. One seeks for itself, the other sacrifices for another.

Read Mark 10:35–45.

Perhaps the root of the problem is revealed in the first phrase, 'we want ...' James and John wanted things to happen their way. The Bible certainly teaches us to ask for things (John 15:16), but the condition is always that we ask 'in His name.' The request of James and John was in their own name, not in His. Sometimes our prayers are just selfish, for personal benefit alone — and this is a good enough reason for God not to answer them — as James explains:

> When you ask, you do not receive, because you ask with wrong motives, that you may spend what you get on your pleasures (James 4:3).

When James and John made their request, they had selfish motives. These are seen in four areas which are common to most of us.

PLEASURE

They wanted to sit either side of Jesus in His glory. As Jews they were no doubt familiar with the rule of King Solomon, whose splendour and riches left the world dazzled. They knew that Jesus would return in glory and perhaps imagined themselves toasting Him with golden goblets filled with the best wine.

Knowing their thoughts, Jesus asked them if they were really able to drink from His cup. Its contents would be hard to swallow, as Jesus discovered in the garden of Gethsemane when His sweat resembled blood and when He pleaded:

> Father, if you are willing, take this cup from me; yet not my will, but yours be done (Luke 22:42).

Serving others is often at the cost of personal pleasure — as Jesus taught in the famous parable of the Good Samaritan (Luke 10:30–35).

I don't think that the Good Samaritan set out that morning with a clear plan to help someone — particularly someone who belonged to a 'despised race'. If we're serious about putting others first, we will often have to make the deliberate decision to deny ourselves for their sake.

POWER

Hunger for power comes almost naturally to us. We like to be in charge. That's why the authority associated with a throne sounds so appealing. James and John probably liked the prospect of wielding power and giving commands which would be instantly obeyed. But power can be dangerous, one reason being that it can give a false sense of confidence and security.

> Read Matthew 7:21–23.
>
> According to Jesus, who will enter the Kingdom of Heaven? How will He respond to some people who claim to have demonstrated great power?

James and John were tempted by power, so was Jesus.

> Read Matthew 4:8–10.
>
> What was Jesus offered? What was the condition? What did Jesus choose to do instead?

Jesus refused to fall for the splendour and trappings of power. Instead He chose to serve God. This was His radical prescription for success:

> **whoever wants to become great among you must be your servant, and whoever wants to be first must be slave of all (Mark 10:43–44).**

PRESTIGE

Besides pleasure and power, a throne gives a tremendous sense of prestige. It is a place where someone receives honour, respect and reverence. Did James and John have this in mind too? If so, it would have contradicted Jesus' understanding of prestige. He didn't grasp for recognition and respect, but promoted the interests of others before His own.

> [He] made himself nothing, taking the very nature of a servant (Phil. 2:7).

The presence of competition reveals how strong our desire for prestige really is. There's glamour attached to winning anything, and Christians often rush for it as quickly as unbelievers. The Christian attitude should resemble that shown by Abram who discovered his herdsmen locked in a quarrel with those of his nephew, Lot.

> Read Genesis 13:5–11.

> Consider Abram's attitude. How did Lot make his choice? (v. 10)

Like Lot, we often choose the best for ourselves. Jesus already had the best — He was equal to God! But He refused to cling to it. Christians live for Him, not for themselves. They lay aside the desire for prestige and recognition and are simply happy to serve.

Another danger for Christians lies in the area of self-vindication. When we are accused of something that we haven't done, we rush to protect ourselves. In fact, we're often quick to do that when we're in the wrong as well! Somehow we feel that we must justify ourselves and protect our reputation.

Pilate was used to seeing people defend their behaviour when they stood before him. We might have expected an innocent Saviour to vindicate Himself very successfully, but He left His case in the hands of God.

Read Mark 15:5 and 1 Peter 2:21–23.

What was Jesus' reaction to accusation? What was Pilate's reaction to Jesus?

Jesus, who made Himself of no reputation, naturally didn't need to defend it. This doesn't mean that we should always remain silent when we are accused or insulted. But it does mean that we must be on our guard against that deep-rooted, selfish streak which is concerned for 'my prestige'.

COMFORT

Lastly, the throne speaks of a very comfortable place which caters for every whim and fancy. To James and John, a throne in heaven must have seemed especially attractive!

If you were in a place of tremendous wealth here on earth, with an unlimited number of servants at your disposal, what practical things would you like them to do for you?
List them on a piece of paper or in a notebook.

Read Matthew 7:12.

How does Jesus sum up the law and the prophets?

This means that everything you have mentioned in your list, you should be able to do for others. God wants you to overcome your desire for personal comfort and to serve others in practical ways.

Go back to your list, write down someone else's name against each job and work out when and how you can do that task for that person.

Good servers must also develop sensitivity. We don't need training to recognise when others don't look after us as we expect. It's obvious. But we do need to be alert to people who are not being treated as they should be. Look around at the end of any church service and you'll notice people who look lost or seem to be hurting. On these, and many other occasions, we should be willing to abandon our desires for fellowship and reach out to satisfy the needs of others. Paul exhorts us:

> Each of you should look not only to your own interests, but also to the interests of others (Phil. 2:4).

Later, Paul describes Timothy as someone who does this.

> I have no-one else like him, who takes a genuine interest in your welfare. For everyone looks out for his own interests, not those of Jesus Christ (Phil. 2:20,21).

When we are acting selfishly and looking after our own interests, we are ignoring the interests of Jesus Christ. His interests are the interests of others.

Chapter Eight

Encouragement

We all know how good it feels when God encourages us. There we are — on the brink of being overwhelmed by our circumstances and almost convinced that no one cares — when suddenly God breaks in to lift our spirits and spur us on. That's exactly what He wants us to do for one another.

What is Encouragement?

The Bible uses the Greek word 'paraclete' to describe an encourager. A paraclete is literally 'one who is called alongside' — a helper. The English word 'encourager' simply means 'one who puts courage in' and could be translated 'fortifier', 'strengthener' or 'comforter'.

God is an encourager in the sense that He is a strengthener. He is 'the God of all comfort, who comforts us in all our troubles' (2 Cor. 1:3,4). Jesus is an encourager, promising that 'I am with you always, to the very end of the age.' (Matt. 28:20). The Holy Spirit is called the Counsellor (Gk. 'Paraclete' in John 14:16). He is with us, strengthens and encourages us.

While the Godhead encourages, the Devil accuses (Rev. 12:10). Day and night he seeks to batter us into discouragement.

Read Hebrews 3:13.

What must we do to avoid hardness of heart?

God doesn't want to see friends merely putting up with one another. He wants us to build each other up through encouragement. There are two aspects to encouragement: appreciation and affirmation.

When we appreciate people, we are recognising something that they've done or a quality that they possess, and we're commending them for it. This is a great stimulus to everyone who is seeking to please God. It's always good to hear a few human 'well dones' before we receive our final commendation from God (Luke 19:17).

When we affirm people, we are building them up before they start a particular venture. We share our faith in them and in their abilities by saying things like: 'Go on, you can do it, I know you can!' This helps them to overcome nervousness and doubt and builds up their confidence for the task ahead.

Read Judges 6:12.

Note the words of affirmation and consider how much encouragement they must have given.

WHAT ENCOURAGEMENT IS NOT

As we seek to build up our friends through encouragement, we must never offer them false reassurances. Encouragement is not:

FLATTERY

We check ourselves for flattery when we ask the question: 'Why am I saying what I'm saying?'

Read through the following list of wrong motives which may cause us to flatter others.
Tick the ones you think you have seen in yourself.

___ It makes me feel good: What a good boy I am! I gave him a few words of encouragement! I was thinking of my benefit, not his.
___ I'm fishing for compliments: If I say nice things about him, perhaps he'll say nice things about me!
___ I'm ingratiating myself: I want him to think I'm a good guy.

____ I need a favour: If I praise him, he might do the same for me.
____ I want to control: I'll butter him up so that he'll do what I want him to do.

We must recognise these wrong motivations and deal with them swiftly. Their intentions are deceptive and carnal. In the short term they may help and encourage others, but they reflect an impure heart attitude and will one day be recognised for what they really are.

UNREALITY

We must not foster pride or false security in our friends by telling them things that simply aren't true, e.g. 'You're going to be a great preacher'. In Jeremiah's time, the people were being told, 'Peace, peace' when there was no peace (Jer. 6:14). This was giving them a false sense of confidence. A true friend doesn't give superficial reassurance, but builds people up so that they can face reality.

THE QUALITIES OF AN ENCOURAGER

Encouragement is such a vital part of New Testament Christianity that the Bible gives us a role model to emulate. His name is Barnabas and we are told in Acts 4:36, the first time he is mentioned, that his name means 'Son of Encouragement'. Let's look at some of the qualities that made him such an effective encourager.

GODLINESS

> Read Acts 11:24 and note the three things that Luke says about Barnabas.

Somebody once remarked:

> **These days, people don't read the Bible. They read the lives of Christians.**

Barnabas practised what he preached and must have been a source of tremendous encouragement to those who knew him.

Is your life characterised by godliness?
Where could you improve?

Of course, Barnabas wasn't perfect. On one occasion he was led astray by the hypocrisy of the Jews (Gal. 2:13). Even though we make mistakes, we can still encourage others.

GIVING

Another mark of encouragers is that they will give as much as they can to help others. Barnabas made quite a spectacular entry into the New Testament when he:

> sold a field he owned and brought the money and put it at the apostles' feet (Acts 4:37).

Giving need not be restricted to money.

On a scale of 0-10 (0=Never; 10=Abundantly), rate your present giving levels with respect to:

Money ____
Time ____
Energy ____
A listening ear ____
A helping hand ____
A bit of advice ____

The act of giving is special because it reflects the character of the One who 'so loved the world that He gave His one and only Son' (John 3:16). If we want to give as God does, we must expect nothing in return and place no conditions on our generosity.

SEEKING GOOD

Encouragers almost automatically do good to others. When Barnabas was in Antioch, he taught the church (Acts 11:26–30). It's likely that his teaching prompted the believers there to give generously to the Jerusalem church while they were going through a time of famine. We should always be looking for opportunities to do good to our friends.

It's possible that Paul learnt the value of encouragement from his friend Barnabas. He encouraged the Philippians to think about things that are true, noble, right, pure, lovely, admirable, excellent or praiseworthy (Phil. 4:8).

There's something in everybody that's worthy of praise. We must just be willing to take the trouble to look for it and comment on it. We should make our encouragement specific. Telling someone that he's 'a great guy' or that she's 'a talented woman' is a good start, but it is much better to say, 'I really appreciate the way you give yourself to help people in need. I've noticed your outstanding patience and tenderness.'

I've found that if I start a sentence with a phrase like, 'I really appreciate the way you ...' or 'What I really admire in you is ...', then I am disciplined to focus on exactly what I do respect in a person. It helps my encouragement to be specific and strengthening.

TEAMWORK

Another quality of encouragers is their desire to work as part of a team and not as individuals. They aren't interested in furthering their own positions. Wherever Barnabas went, he was content to help others to find God's will for their lives.

> He brought a great number into the church in Antioch (Acts 11:24).
> He brought Paul from Tarsus and saw him develop a teaching ministry (Acts 11:25).

He raised up a team of prophets and teachers (Acts 13:1).
He allowed Paul to take over leadership from him (Acts 13:13).
He worked with Mark (Acts 15:39).

THE RESULTS OF ENCOURAGEMENT

Barnabas' encouragement affected many individuals in the New Testament.

PAUL

As a relatively new Christian, the apostle Paul came to Jerusalem to join the disciples.

Read about this in Acts 9:26,27 and note:

The reaction of the disciples there. Why they reacted in this way? Who came to his rescue and how?

A little later Barnabas went to Tarsus to look for Paul and take him to Antioch. We read that:

for a whole year Barnabas and Saul met with the church and taught great numbers of people (Acts 11:26).

Once Barnabas had taken Paul under his wing, he began to establish him as a teacher. When the Spirit set them apart for a special work (Acts 13:1–3), Barnabas, who is mentioned first, was evidently the leader. Then in Acts 13:7,42, the order of the men's names is reversed. Barnabas had clearly encouraged Paul so effectively that he was now the key leader.

MARK

Barnabas also encouraged John Mark. He had been Barnabas and Saul's helper on the first missionary journey, but had abandoned them at Pamphylia (Acts 13:5,13). When they were about to embark on their next major journey, Barnabas viewed Mark differently from Paul.

> Read Acts 15:37–39.
>
> Why did Paul object to John Mark coming along again? What was Barnabas' reaction?

Because he was an encourager, Barnabas was willing to stand by someone who had let him down. Indeed, the encouragement was so effective, that Paul later wrote to Timothy:

> Get Mark and bring him with you, because he is helpful to me in my ministry (2 Tim. 4:11).

IN ANTIOCH

Barnabas' ability to encourage wasn't limited to individuals. He also used it to bless entire churches. When those in the Jerusalem church heard how the gospel was spreading in Antioch, they wanted to find out more and sent Barnabas along. We read:

> When he arrived and saw the evidence of the grace of God, he was glad and encouraged them all to remain true to the Lord with all their hearts (Acts 11:23).

His encouragement resulted in:

> a great number of people [being] brought to the Lord (Acts 11:24).

It wasn't long before Barnabas was leading a team of prophets and teachers in Antioch (Acts 13:1). The whole church flourished through his encouragement.

APPLICATION

Though we may not all have the gifts that Barnabas had, we all can encourage our friends in ways we've seen in this study.

Read Hebrews 10:24,25.

What three things do these verses tell us to do?

We are encouraged to be encouragers — which will require deliberate effort on each one's part. Here are a few ideas you might like to use as you seek to encourage:

Come alongside. Simply being there is encouraging.
Speak words of appreciation and affirmation.
Write letters/notes/cards.
Offer hospitality.
Give a gift or a bunch of flowers.
Make a phone call, possibly a long distance one.
Visit, especially at a time of need.
Pray.

Be generous in your encouragement. Try to support, reassure and build up. Remember, as you take steps to do this, encouraging will become a habit.

Write down the names of three friends and make a note of how you can encourage each of them in a specific area.

Chapter Nine

OPENNESS

Transparency is a hallmark of the Kingdom. When God revealed the New Jerusalem to the apostle John, He showed him that:

> the great street of the city was of pure gold, like transparent glass (Rev. 21:21).

We may be able to hide things from others on earth, but nothing will be hidden in heaven. Jesus warned His disciples about this when He said:

> There is nothing concealed that will not be disclosed, or hidden that will not be made known (Matt. 10:26).

When we pray for the Kingdom to come on earth 'as it is in heaven' we are asking, among other things, for God to establish transparency in our lives. Openness is not an end in itself. It helps us to develop maturity in our relationships with God and others. Of course, God knows everything about us, including our deepest thoughts and attitudes, but He is looking for a people who are growing in openness — men and women who do not even try to keep secrets from one another. Jesus, the ruler of this Kingdom, sets the example of openness. When He was on earth, He shared His life with twelve men whom He called His friends.

Read John 15:15.

Why did Jesus call them His friends?

Jesus used the word, 'everything' to describe what He told His disciples. He also said that His Spirit would guide them into all truth, and that He Himself was the truth. He was so open that He could say to Philip:

> Anyone who has seen me has seen the Father (John 14:9).

Friendships in the Kingdom should be genuine, committed and constantly deepening. That being the case, we must see openness as a priority, not as an optional extra. Only as we show our 'real' selves to our friends can we enjoy relationships which are without pretence or disguise.

Several years ago, two American sociologists developed the concept of the 'Johari Window' which basically shows all that I am under four areas:

The things I know about me.
The things I don't know about me.
The things others know about me.
The things others don't know about me.

They included the information in a 'window' which looks like this:

The four areas of 'me':

EXPRESSING	Known to me	Unknown to me
Unknown to others	Secrets	Totally unknown except to God
Known to others	'Common' knowledge	Blindspots

LISTENING

Let's look briefly at these four areas.

'COMMON' KNOWLEDGE

Everything in this area is known to me and also to others. Indeed, it also tends to be obvious to anybody who's interested. It includes anything from a long nose to a habit like smoking.

Consider three things in your life that you would classify under 'Common' knowledge.

SECRETS

This area covers things that we know to be true about ourselves but have not mentioned to anybody else, except perhaps God. Here, we would find things like inner struggles and loneliness.

Consider a time when you kept something a 'secret' for a long time, but finally shared it with a friend. How did you feel once you'd revealed your secret?

BLINDSPOTS

These are actions, habits or character deficiencies of which we are oblivious unless they're pointed out. It could be something like scratching your head, picking your nose, constantly turning everything into a joke, and treating a person badly.

Consider a time when someone pointed out something in your life which you had not noticed before.

TOTALLY UNKNOWN

These are areas in our lives that remain unknown both to us and to others. God alone is aware of them, yet He still loves and accepts us as we are.

The Johari Window is different for each of us, and also varies with time. For example a person who talks freely about himself, but is unwilling to listen to any correction or criticism, would have a diagram like this:

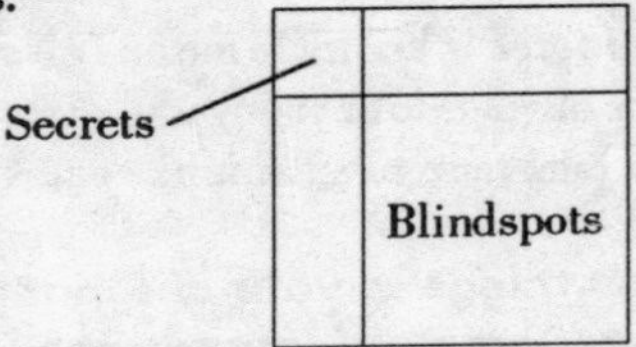

A person who is very receptive to what others have to say about him, but who tends to bottle things up inside, would have a diagram like this:

The Johari Window is also a way of looking at our spiritual maturity. As we become more like Jesus, we will have fewer 'secrets' and 'blindspots'. As Paul says:

> Now I know in part; then I shall know fully, even as I am fully known (1 Cor. 13:12).

In heaven we'll be free of secrets and blindspots for ever. To get us ready for that time, we need to work at two things:

Expressing ourselves openly to reduce our secrets.
Listening to others openly to reduce our blindspots.

Why not complete your own personal Johari Window by rating yourself from 0 to 10 in both these two areas:

Expressing openly _____ and Listening _____.

Then draw the lines on the following graph.

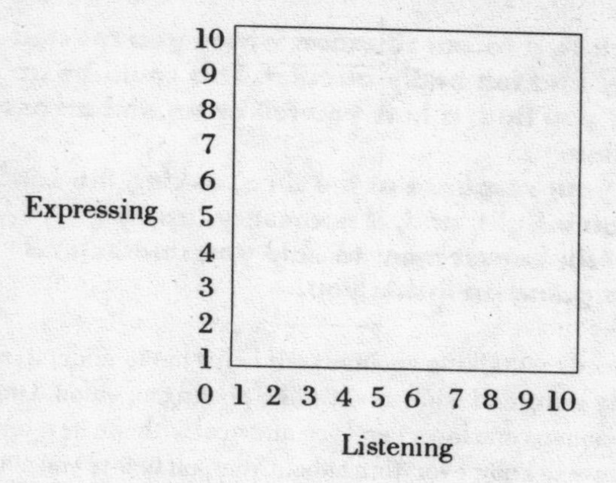

EXPRESSING OURSELVES OPENLY

For most of us, openness doesn't come easily. It would be great if we could become Christlike simply by reading books, praying, or meditating on the Bible. But God's maturing process involves people and many of us have to work at opening ourselves up to them. I recognise three main obstacles to openness in my life.

I JUST DON'T KNOW MYSELF

Quite often I can't be open about myself because I don't know what's going on inside me. I don't know why I reacted like that, spoke those words, felt so disturbed. At times like these, I find it helpful to apply Rudyard Kipling's poem:

> I keep six honest, serving-men
> (They taught me all I knew);
> Their names are What and Why and When
> And How and Where and Who.[1]

If we develop a habit of asking ourselves questions, we are more likely to understand why we act, speak, think and feel as we do. Only then can we start being open about what's going on.

Think back to a recent situation where you reacted negatively and felt badly about it. This could be an argument you had, a hurt you felt or an embarrassing situation.
Consider your response at the time, asking the Lord to give you insight, and, if necessary, apply Kipling's 'six honest men' to help you understand what was going on inside you.

I've noticed that talking about myself helps me to understand what's really going on inside me. It's like peeling an onion. Only when I've removed one layer can I see and deal with the next one. You don't have to know everything about yourself before you start opening up. I am not, of course, advocating morbid introspection, but as I have gone on in my Christian life, I have found that there are always further areas of my inner life which the Lord wants to uncover and deal with. And it almost always helps me if I talk about them to a trusted friend.

I DON'T THINK PEOPLE WILL BE INTERESTED

I once felt so inferior and inadequate that I thought nobody could possibly be interested in what I had to say. There seemed to be so many other people who had far more interesting stories than me — and they could tell them with such excitement that everyone around was spellbound. While they got the attention, I retreated into shyness and locked the door behind me.

When the Lord began setting me free, he helped me to see that I'm His unique creation with unique gifts. He also revealed that He's taken me through things — both before and after I became a Christian — which others will find interesting and helpful. Our treasure is in earthen vessels, and sometimes we need to display it.

If you feel that no one is interested in what you have to say, ask God to forgive you, and to help you to express your feelings when you're with your friends.

I'M AFRAID TO BE OPEN

Even if we know ourselves quite well and think people might be interested in us, we can still find it difficult to share openly about ourselves. This is because we're afraid of saying the wrong thing or of having people look down on us. Our pride works hard at protecting us from embarrassment.

Adam and Eve showed their fear of being open by covering themselves with fig leaves and hiding from God (Gen. 3:7–10). They have passed down to us the instinct to run and hide. But, as I once heard someone comment, 'Saving us from embarrassment is not very high on God's list of priorities.' In fact He uses our embarrassment to dig deeper into our lives.

God wants us to take bold strides towards more open friendships. I find that on occasions I have to make a very deliberate decision to talk about certain things to a friend — particularly if those things put me in a negative light. Everything within me resists the idea of transparency, but I take the plunge because I'm learning the importance of being open and vulnerable. It helps to remember that God knows everything about me and still loves me just as I am.

Do you fear that people will find out about an embarrassing secret in your life?
Ask God to show you someone with whom you can share it.

---

[1] Taken from *The Elephant's Child* by Rudyard Kipling.

Chapter Ten

LISTENING

Openness and listening are two vital ingredients for our spiritual growth. If we listen to what others say about us, we will learn about our blindspots and will then be able to deal with them. Attentive listening is also regarded by experts as one of the best ways of making friends. A lonely person will be really encouraged when he discovers someone who is simply willing to listen to him.

The Bible is called the 'Word of God' because God speaks to us through it. But God isn't just a speaker, He's a listener too.

> Does he who implanted the ear not hear? Does he who formed the eye not see? (Ps. 94:9)

We are able to listen only because God is a listener and has given us ears. He is quick to listen to everything we say — whether privately to Him, or in everyday conversations with others.

THE PROCESS OF LISTENING

Listening involves more than many of us think. It isn't just hearing, which is the physical process by which we pick up sound waves. Rather, it includes understanding (and sometimes misunderstanding) of information which has been heard, interpretation, evaluation and finally action.

Understanding plays a key role in listening. Jesus told the parable of the sower to show that the Word of God has different effects on different people (Matt. 13:18–23). If you read this passage, you will notice that the seed which is snatched away applies to a person who has heard but not understood the message (v. 19). The seed which bears fruit has been both heard and understood (v. 23).

THE PRACTICE OF LISTENING

Good listening requires effort. We must give careful attention to what and how we hear. After Mark's account of the parable of the sower, Jesus warns us:

> Consider carefully what you hear ... With the measure you use, it will be measured to you — and even more (Mark 4:24).

What are some of the 'measures' that we can use when we listen to others?

LISTENING FOR FAULTS

Many of us tend to listen with a judgemental attitude. Jesus warns us:

> Do not judge, or you too will be judged. For in the same way as you judge others, you will be judged, and with the measure you use, it will be measured to you (Matt. 7:1,2).

It is very easy to adopt a critical and cynical attitude to others — whether they're speaking publicly or in a private setting. The unhealthy desire to pick out others' faults gets in the way of real listening. Even if the person's accent or grammar is strange or his story offensive, it isn't our job to judge, but to listen with interest and compassion.

LISTENING FOR OUR OWN DESIRES

Paul knew that we would be tempted to listen only to the things that appealed to us, so he warns us:

> For the time will come when men will not put up with sound doctrine. Instead, to suit their own desires, they will gather around them a great number of teachers to say what their itching ears want to hear. They will turn their ears away from the truth and turn aside to myths (2 Tim. 4:3,4).

This solemn warning shows that the way we listen can determine whether we live according to sound doctrine or myths. Some people preach very attractive messages which appeal to our selfish instincts, but which are useless to us.

Even in everyday conversations we must be on our guard against selfish listening. Sometimes we are too concerned about how we feel (bored, amused, shocked, etc.) that we totally fail to hear and understand all that the other person is trying to express.

LISTENING TO GOSSIP

Gossip could be defined as any unnecessary talk (whether true or false) about a third party. It has always been a very attractive pastime. Somebody only has to say, 'Did you hear what happened to ...?' and every ear in the room springs to attention. Solomon said:

> The words of a gossip are like choice morsels; they go down to a man's inmost parts (Prov. 18:8).

It's almost impossible not to be affected by gossip. That's why it's so dangerous. When we hear something said against a person, the words get deep into our spirits and it's very hard to clear them out.

We must make a conscious decision not to listen to gossip. This means that when someone is talking about someone else, we should be asking ourselves, 'What's his motive for sharing that?' If he is trying to put down the third party, then we're encouraging gossip by listening to him and must graciously but firmly refuse to listen to it.

Consider a recent occasion when you were guilty of listening to gossip.
If you haven't done so already, ask God to forgive you.

LISTENING FOR MERE INFORMATION

Another famous way of deceiving others is to listen simply to accumulate knowledge. In the parable of the wise and foolish builders, both men heard Jesus' words, but only one put them into practice (Matt. 7:24–27). Only when we apply what we hear will our 'house' stand in the storms. Information without action gives us a deceptive sense of security, as James underlines:

> Do not merely listen to the word, and so deceive yourselves. Do what it says (James 1:22).

LISTENING FOR THE GOOD OF THE SPEAKER

God wants us to listen as He does. The right 'measure' concerns our being more interested in the good of the person who's speaking than in anything else. Here are a few tips as to how we can do this:

Look interested: make eye contact, nod your head in agreement, respond with facial expressions.
Inquire with questions: use sensitive questions to draw the person out and help him to open up.
Stay on target: don't let the conversation ramble but lovingly bring it back.
Test your understanding: occasionally summarise in your own words what you think the person has said.
Evaluate the message: consider it from different angles and try to see what he's really saying.

Neutralise your feelings: ask the Lord for self-control so that your emotions don't get in the way.

THE TEST OF LISTENING

The way that we respond to feedback about ourselves is a good test of our ability to listen. Having looked at the Johari window in Chapter Nine, we all should be aware that we have blindspots, but most of us find it hard to really listen when somebody actually tries to point one out.

For example, a man may have bored people for years, but when a loving friend informs him that he's a bore, he will quickly retort, 'How dare you? I've been speaking this way for ages and no one has ever hinted that I'm boring.' The truth is that no one who'd been with him before had ever mustered the courage to tell him the truth.

When a friend points out a blindspot that I've unknowingly had for years, I rarely respond with heartfelt appreciation! This sort of feedback doesn't come naturally or easily to me — as my wife would quickly tell you. But I'm slowly learning the importance of being an open listener. The Bible reveals four ways in which I can respond to correction.

HATRED

'Don't tell me what to do, I'm the captain of this ship and I'll run it as I want!' The Bible warns us of the consequences of a response like this.

> Read Proverbs 15:10 and note what happens to someone who hates correction.

The death that's described here will more often be spiritual than physical. Sadly the Christian world is full of the living bodies of people who have refused to heed correction. They never enjoy the kind of abundant life that Jesus promised because they stubbornly resist knowing anything about themselves that smacks of criticism.

Read Proverbs 12:1 and note how the Bible describes those who don't like correction.

Pray now that God will help you to be more willing to receive correction.

MAKING LIGHT

'Oh yes, I know I'm doing that, but so is everyone else. Anyway, we all make mistakes.' This is a useful, but ungodly way to avoid admitting wrong. The writer to the Hebrews warns us about 'making light' of the Lord's discipline (Heb. 12:5). Laughing away admonition puts off the need to repent or change.

Read Proverbs 9:7,8 and note what these verses say about a mocker.

These verses tell us that a mocker is anybody who insults or hates a person who has corrected or rebuked him. 'He said it in the wrong way,' the corrected man declares. 'The timing was inappropriate' or 'He's often mistaken about other things.' If we mock or make light of correction we might be able to cover up our unwillingness to face up to the truth about ourselves. Jamie Buckingham wrote, 'A man doesn't have to be a butcher to tell if a steak tastes good or bad.'[1] Someone who corrects me may well have expressed himself better and chosen a more appropriate time. He may also be mistaken about many things, but he can still give me helpful correction. Rather than mock him and excuse myself, I must listen to the content of what he's saying and respond to that. God wants me to change my character not my corrector!

DISCOURAGEMENT

'What's the use? I'll never change. I might as well give up.' That's the response of a discouraged person. Having warned us not to make light of the Lord's discipline, the writer to the Hebrews warns us against another common reaction:

> **do not lose heart when he rebukes you (Heb. 12:5).**

Discouragement is probably the most usual reaction to correction. We start by feeling generally hopeless and sorry for ourselves, and before we know it, we're indulging in feelings of rejection and self-pity. Then we think that we might as well give up altogether.

> Read Hebrews 12:6 and note why we should not become discouraged.

Correction is proof that God accepts and loves us. It's hard to remember this just after we've been rebuked. But if in future 'correction situations' we discipline our minds to think of this Scripture rather than look at ourselves, we will be full of encouragement, not despair.

RESPONSIVENESS

There are great benefits to heeding and acting on correction. If we respond positively, we will be enriched personally and strengthened in our relationships with others.

> Read Proverbs 13:18 and 15:32 and note the benefits of listening to correction.

> Ask God to help you to be a better listener — especially in situations where He wants you to receive correction.

I once read this statement:

> If you knew I wouldn't get defensive or angry, what hard truth would you like to tell me? Is there something you've been wanting to say to me, but haven't dared to because you were afraid of my reaction? Well, now's your chance.[2]

Sit down with a friend ask him or her this question. It won't be easy, but it will be an excellent way of removing blindspots and helping you to grow in maturity.

ARE YOU LISTENING?

Rate yourself on a scale of 0 to 10 on the following ten areas of listening:
0 = almost always you're like the bad listener
5 = sometimes you're bad, sometimes you're good
10 = almost always you're like the good listener
Circle the number which you feel reflects your level of listening skill in each area.

THE BAD LISTENER	THE GOOD LISTENER
1. Switches off for dry subjects — sees them as boring or uninteresting.	1. Finds areas of interest. Asks, 'What's in this for me?'

Bad 0 1 2 3 4 5 6 7 8 9 10 Good

THE BAD LISTENER	THE GOOD LISTENER
2. Switches off if delivery is poor. Criticises speaker's delivery or mannerisms.	2. Judges content. Does not bother about delivery or presentation errors.

Bad 0 1 2 3 4 5 6 7 8 9 10 Good

3. Gets over-excited and tends to enter into argument.	3. Doesn't judge until he has fully understood the speaker's point.

Bad 0 1 2 3 4 5 6 7 8 9 10 Good

4. Listens only to facts.	4. Listens for ideas and central themes.

Bad 0 1 2 3 4 5 6 7 8 9 10 Good

5. Takes intensive notes using only one system but often misses main point.	5. Takes fewer notes but uses different systems for different speakers.

Bad 0 1 2 3 4 5 6 7 8 9 10 Good

6. Shows little energy output. Only pretends to pay attention.	6. Works hard at listening. Body movements show he is interested.

Bad 0 1 2 3 4 5 6 7 8 9 10 Good

7. Allows distractions to quickly take away attention.	7. Fights or avoids distractions. Knows how to concentrate.

Bad 0 1 2 3 4 5 6 7 8 9 10 Good

8. Switches off when material is heavy or complicated. Seeks light, amusing material.	8. Uses heavier material exercise to discipline and stimulate the mind.

Bad 0 1 2 3 4 5 6 7 8 9 10 Good

9. Reacts to emotional words and feels personally antagonistic to speaker.

9. Interprets 'colour' words and does not get hung up on them.

Bad 0 1 2 3 4 5 6 7 8 9 10 Good

10. Tends to daydream with slow speaker.

10. Uses fact that thought is faster than speech to anticipate, summarise, weigh evidence and listen to tone of voice.

Bad 0 1 2 3 4 5 6 7 8 9 10 Good

---

[1] *Coping with Criticism* by Jamie Buckingham. © 1978 Logos International.

[2] *Honest to God?* by Bill Hybels. © 1990 by Bill Hybels. Used by permission of Zondervan Publishing House.

Chapter Eleven

ADMONITION

Most of us were happy to leave admonition behind when we left school. It sounds too painful to resurrect in the present. But admonition is not only a test of true friendship, it is also a biblical principle.

> Wounds from a friend can be trusted, but an enemy multiplies kisses (Prov. 27:6).

> Let the word of Christ dwell in you richly as you teach and admonish one another with all wisdom (Col. 3:16).

'Admonish' literally means 'to put into another's mind' and it's essential if we want to deepen our characters and friendships. At times it will include correction and confrontation, but its aim is always to build people up and steer them away from wrong.

> Read Galatians 6:1 and note how we should restore someone who has fallen.

You might think, 'It's unfair to go around correcting folks who don't see eye to eye with us'. You're dead right! We admonish others only if we are seeking to uphold a value from the Bible. And we can only teach and admonish if the Word dwells in us (Col. 3:16).

When we confront our friends we must avoid the danger of looking at their faults and failing to examine our own motives and actions. Jesus warned us:

Why do you look at the speck of sawdust in your brother's eye and pay no attention to the plank in your own eye? (Matt. 7:3)

THE BENEFITS OF ADMONITION

If you skim through the last few chapters of Mark, you will see how quick Jesus was to admonish others. Here are a few instances which allow us to see how helpful admonition can be.

IT EXPOSES PROBLEMS

Read Mark 9:33–35.

Note the problem and how Jesus corrected it.

When Jesus suspected that something wasn't quite right, He asked a question. This effectively notified the disciples that they had a problem — which is why they kept quiet. Jesus then took the opportunity to teach them the godly perspective of greatness.

Sometimes, by talking openly to a person who has hurt me, I discover that I've been upset because I've made all sorts of false assumptions. On occasions I've genuinely misunderstood something, or have been unaware of the background to a comment. If I then refuse to confront, I will probably hold onto my wrong thoughts and the relationship will turn sour. But the asking of a simple question exposes my mistake and brings healing.

IT SETS STANDARDS AND LIMITS

Read Mark 10:13,14.

Whom did Jesus rebuke and why?

The disciples obviously hadn't understood how highly God valued children. Jesus' rebuke made them aware of their error.

In our early days in Bombay, people were shocked when at 7.30 p.m. I excused myself from talking to church members and went off to read a story to my children. When I explained my priority commitment to the children, I was effectively rebuking the frequent lack of concern for young people in India and demonstrating a different standard for fathering.

IT REINFORCES BIBLE TEACHING

Read Mark 10:17,18.

Which Bible value do you think that Jesus was trying to communicate?

When we point out or question words or actions which fall short of God's standard, we are teaching people about God — sometimes for the first time.

IT DEEPENS AND STRENGTHENS RELATIONSHIPS

Read Mark 16:14.

Why does Jesus rebuke His disciples here?

The book of Acts tells us that after this rebuke these same men went on to serve the Lord passionately. They all responded with such enthusiasm that most of them ended up dying for Jesus.

HOW DO I ADMONISH?

This is where we feel uncomfortable! Admonishing a friend is quite difficult. We can do it in a number of different ways.

THE POLICEMAN

This admonisher will not stand for any nonsense! He sees the wrong, calls it a crime and prescribes the appropriate and immediate punishment. They resemble James and John who were ready to punish with fire. Clearly they had no compassion for the Samaritans (Luke 9:51–56). It's God's responsibility to punish the guilty, not ours. We just point out sin.

THE LAWYER

This admonisher has no sympathy whatsoever. His dossier is brimming with evidence for guilt and he argues his case with logic and reason. 'Is it not true that on the night of the 25th you ...' Our job is to pinpoint wrong, not to bring a Perry Mason style verdict. Once again, it's God who convicts.

THE 'SOFT' COUNSELLOR

This person is so polite and gentle that the person admonished never realises that he has actually sinned. The 'soft' counsellor avoids pinpointing wrong and muffles the stark truth with expressions like: 'perhaps you could have ...', 'maybe you ought ...' and 'Don't you think you ...' Jesus would never have fudged issues like that! He tells the Laodicean church:

> **Those whom I love I rebuke and discipline. So be earnest, and repent (Rev. 3:19).**

THE MANIPULATOR

This admonisher is using admonition to get his or her own way. He will use admonition to play on the listener's emotions, but his real desire is to get what he wants.

> Read Judges 16:15–17 to see how successfully Delilah used (or misused) admonition.

THE MEDIATOR

This is the true friend. He tries to reconcile the wrongdoer to God without any thought of personal gain or cost. When David committed adultery with Bathsheba and arranged for the murder of her husband, Nathan confronted him.

> Read 2 Samuel 12:1–10.

Nathan gives us an excellent example of how to admonish. Lets look at this.

He had a relationship with David

Read 2 Samuel 7:1–3.

The Bible doesn't teach us that the way to 'admonish' is to 'blast off' at people. It's something that's done gently, preferably out of relationship — although we will sometimes need to rebuke someone who is almost a stranger to us. Whenever we challenge someone, we must first assess the strength or weakness of the relationship, because that will usually determine how much we can say.

We must remember that leaders sometimes need to be admonished too. If you think that you need to talk to someone in authority over you, do that — but be sure you maintain a gracious, submissive spirit. A godly leader will be grateful to you for your courage in being open with him.

The Lord wanted him to admonish David

Obviously, Nathan had been praying about the situation and God had told him to go to David. It's always hard to know whether God wants you to admonish someone. For this reason, many Christians shrug off something when they should be confronting it. When we know that God wants us to challenge someone, we should always check out our proposed correction against the Word of God.

Read 2 Timothy 3:16.

What is all Scripture useful for? (Note especially those middle two! We tend to forget them.)

He'd thought it through

Nathan wasn't carried away by emotion. Instead, he told a well thought out story which stirred David's anger. Jesus tells us exactly how to confront someone who has sinned against us:

> **go and show him his fault, just between the two of you. If he listens to you, you have won your brother over (Matt. 18:15).**

The goal of all admonishing is to win over the other person.

Read Matthew 18:16, 17 and note what to do if this action doesn't work.

He talked directly to David

Read 2 Samuel 12:7.

What did Nathan say to David?

Confrontation is about proclaiming the truth. Paul had to do this.

Read Galatians 2:11–13 and note Peter's problem and Paul's response.

In this case, the confrontation was public because the sin affected the whole church.

He had faith for the situation

When Nathan received God's message, it's likely that he waited for the right time before he went to David with it. It's also probable that he believed that God would open David's heart to the correction.

Not everybody responds as quickly as David. Some people need a year (or more) before they're willing to acknowledge that the correction really was from God. Indeed, some people who react too quickly have not actually been convicted of sin and fail to go through a time of genuine repentance. We must not be over-concerned about the immediate reaction. It's our job just to keep trusting and praying.

When someone can't receive the admonition, we must leave the door open so that we can talk further at some future date. It isn't appropriate to say, 'That's it. I never want to see you again.' If you do that, you're the one who will have to go back and ask for forgiveness — or wait for a Nathan to come and admonish you!

Thankfully, David recognised his sin and made a clear confession. So Nathan pronounced:

> The LORD has taken away your sin. You are not going to die (2 Sam. 12:13).

When we confront our friends, our goal should be to restore them to godly behaviour. If they receive our correction, we would expect them to:

Confess their sin to God and ask for His forgiveness.
Confess their sin to all who have been affected by it.
Declare their intention not to sin in this way again.
Make appropriate restitution, including restoring a person's reputation if it has been damaged.

Look at the list of different admonishing styles and tick which of them most resembles you. (You may find yourself in more than one category.)

___ Policeman
___ Lawyer
___ 'Soft' Counsellor
___ Manipulator
___ Mediator

Recall a recent incident where you now feel you did not admonish a friend appropriately.
How would you have handled it now?
Is there anything you could do now?
Pray for guidance if necessary.

Chapter Twelve

Togetherness

God the Father, Son and Holy Spirit work and relate together in perfect harmony. This is the model for Christian friendship which we are called to demonstrate to an impersonal world.

The Father and Son were together in the beginning and made everything between them (John 1:1–3). Their relationship involved being and doing. Jesus was born and grew up in the context of a family. He would have related to His parents, brothers and sisters and helped around the house and in the carpenter's shop. He would not have been a loner. When Jesus started His public ministry, He chose friends to be with Him and to help Him.

Consider the sort of things that friends do together to help build their friendship.
If you're doing this study in a group, take turns at giving ideas. You'll be amazed at how imaginative you can be as you work together!

I found six main headings in the gospels that indicate the range of activities which Jesus and His friends enjoyed together.

Eating

There are many accounts of Jesus eating meals with His friends. There's something special about sharing food together. It's a sort of bonding. That's why David was so shocked when:

Even my close friend, whom I trusted, he who shared my bread, has lifted up his heel against me (Ps. 41:9).

Jesus and His disciples shared meals in a variety of ways. For a start, they went out to other people's homes.

Read Luke 5:38,39 and 10:38–42.

Whose homes were these?

The disciples (and possibly Jesus) also enjoyed some 'snacks' (Luke 6:1–5) and catered for two vast crowds (Mark 6:33–44; 8:1–9). But it was Jesus and His twelve closest friends who ate the Last Supper together (Luke 22:8).

Read John 4:8.

Who went to get the food?

Read John 21:12,13.

Who prepared breakfast?

Clearly, Jesus enjoyed a variety of 'eating experiences' with His friends. We could add our own ideas to them — picnics, barbecues and 'bring a dish'. Friends should use meal times as much as possible to build and strengthen their relationships. The food is not as vital as the conversation and sense of togetherness.

LEARNING

Jesus devoted a large proportion of His life to teaching His disciples. Learning together builds Christian friendships in any context — sacred or secular. It also motivates us to press on.

Consider embarking on a course with a friend or two. You could work through a study guide or a series of church-run teaching sessions. Or you could enrol on a course at a local school, college or leisure centre, or join an outside training programme.

MEETING GOD

It should be natural for Christians to meet God together. Jesus prayed publicly with His disciples (Luke 11:1; John 17). Friends should be quick to pray with and for each other.

> Read Matthew 18:19,20 and note the two significant promises that Jesus made.

Jesus was keen to have His closest friends with Him when He went up a mountain to pray (Luke 9:28–35). Peter, James and John had an overwhelming experience on that mountain. Shared experiences like this are exciting and edifying for God's people. It's good for friends to meet to:

Worship God.
Pray for the sick.
Attend Bible Weeks.
Go evangelising.
Fast and pray.
Break bread.
Cast out demons.
Visit the elderly/those in prison.
Move in Spiritual gifts — tongues, prophecy, etc.

TRAVELLING

Jesus was continually travelling with his friends, and presumably stayed in different places with them. Sometimes they were in a boat (Luke 8:22–25), on other occasions they were simply walking together (Luke 9:57).

I've found that travelling together is a great opportunity for building friendships — especially on Indian trains, because they try to pack as many hours as possible into the distance covered!

The next time you have to travel somewhere, why not see if you can take a friend with you and use the journey to get to know each other better? Maybe you could even plan a holiday with a friend.

WORKING

Another great way of building friendships is to do practical things together. I've enjoyed some really fulfilling and productive times, working with others at things like:

Washing up.
Repairing the car.
Putting in new plumbing.
Helping to move house.
Painting furniture.
Building a cupboard.
Doing the garden.
Cleaning the house.
Cooking a meal.
Painting a room.

For the world, the motto is: 'Do It Yourself'. For Christians, this would be far better rendered: 'Do It Together'.

We can't be sure if Jesus ever went fishing with His 'fishermen' friends, but He was certainly fully involved with them and gave them some excellent advice. When they hadn't caught any fish, He told them:

Throw your net on the right side of the boat and you will find some (John 21:6).

God wants us to include Him in our work as individuals and also in our group settings.

Think of a time when you were able to work alongside a friend.
What were the benefits for you?

CELEBRATING

Jesus enjoyed celebrating with His friends. He was the guest of honour at Levi's banquet (Luke 5:29,30) and went with His disciples to the wedding at Cana (John 2:1ff).

It's good to hold lively celebrations when there's a special occasion like a birthday or a wedding anniversary. Celebrations demonstrate our love and respect for people and they go down particularly well if we include one or more of the following:

SURPRISE

It's worth all the planning and secrecy to see a friend's mouth drop in utter amazement as they discover that a surprise event has been arranged for them.

ENTERTAINMENT

Live entertainment by gifted friends is the most enjoyable. But it's also fun to entertain friends through TV, videos, sporting events, theatre, etc.

GAMES

Most people enjoy playing games together. These games can include outdoor sports or indoor activities. I've found it helpful to write down ideas for games that work so that I can produce them at the appropriate time.

LAUGHTER

All friendships need to include laughter. I really enjoy a good laugh with my closest friends and I'd encourage you to welcome times of good fun. The Bible is silent about whether or not Jesus laughed, but He certainly rejoiced with exceeding joy, which must surely surpass it.

Think of two or three people with whom you'd like to enjoy closer friendships.
In each case, what could you actually do together to build that friendship?

Chapter Thirteen

Handling Disagreements

Sooner or later in every friendship, there will be a disagreement. Jesus knew this and taught His disciples how to put things right. One of the most famous Bible disagreements is recorded painfully and honestly in the book of Acts.

Read Acts 15:36–41.

Going Wrong

If Paul and Barnabas could have such a sharp disagreement, after all they'd done together, the same could happen to us. Before we look at how to put disagreements right, let's see, with reference to Paul and Barnabas, why things go wrong.

BOTH WERE RIGHT!

Each man had good, Scriptural reasons to support his point of view. You can imagine them arguing along these lines:

Paul — Let's not take John Mark with us. He's a liability! Walked out on us in Pamphylia (Acts 13:13). Deserted us when we really needed his help.

Barnabas — But he's got real potential! I'm sure God can use him mightily (2 Tim. 4:11).

Paul — Potential is not the issue. He let us down badly. Come to think of it, so did you (Gal. 2:13). You've got something in common!

Barnabas — Come on, now. I was the one who picked you up and got you into the ministry in the first place (Acts 9:27; 11:25,26).

Paul — But now it's hard for you to accept my anointing and leadership, isn't it? (Acts 13:42)

Barnabas — Of course not! Didn't you notice how they asked me to speak first in Jerusalem? (Acts 15:12) All you want is to have things your way.

Paul — You take him, then. I'm off with Silas!

Maybe it wasn't as bad as this, but it was certainly a sharp disagreement.

BOTH WERE SURE THEY WERE RIGHT!

Each of them was so sure of his point of view that he refused to listen to the other (remember the chapter on listening?). This is familiar territory. In times of conflict, few of us are really willing to listen to the other person. We see things in black and white and assume that if we're right, then the other must be wrong. Life isn't always that simple.

BOTH REACTED BADLY!

The disagreement was so sharp that they parted company. Barnabas took Mark and sailed to Cyprus, while Paul went off with Silas. It's likely that while they argued, they both said things that they later regretted and felt rather guilty about. The Bible warns us that:

> When words are many, sin is not absent (Prov. 10:19).
>
> Reckless words pierce like a sword (Prov. 12:18).

Can you think of any time when you said something that you later regretted?
If not, I'm sure you can remember an occasion when somebody said something which really hurt you.

SETTING RIGHT

It's probable that Paul and Barnabas both thought: 'I'm right and I'm hurting.' We don't actually know from the Acts account what they did, but based on New Testament teaching, I imagine that they handled their disagreement by doing what I suggest that you do.

TALK TO JESUS

Whatever the problem and however misunderstood and angry you feel, remember that God knows what you're going through.

> Read Hebrews 4:15,16 and consider:
>
> How Jesus reacts to our weaknesses.
> How we approach the throne of grace.
> What we receive and find in our time of need.

The great temptation is to ignore Jesus and instead talk to others about how we've been hurt. Often we excuse ourselves by saying that all we're looking for is a 'shoulder to cry on'. It's worth remembering the following truth:

> **He who covers over an offence promotes love, but whoever repeats the matter separates close friends (Prov. 17:9).**

Very often we talk after a disagreement because we have a deep longing for somebody to tell us that we're right and that the other person is wrong! The Bible calls this 'gossip' and tells us not to do it. We must beware of self-justification. At His trial Jesus simply remained silent (Mark 14:61) and Paul wrote:

> **The very fact that you have lawsuits among you means you have been completely defeated already (1 Cor. 6:7).**

By trying to win the argument, we demonstrate that we've already lost it. God wants us to be willing to lay down our lives for our friends, not to fight against them.

Jesus must have felt the pain of injustice, but He still controlled His emotions and acted in a godly way. We must not allow our feelings to toss us around. God wants us to receive His inner strength by prayerfully acknowledging:

That His grace is sufficient for us to react to our circumstances with patience, forgiveness and forbearance.

That He is sovereign, has allowed these things to happen and will use them for our good (Rom. 8:28).

BE HONEST

Honesty has always been 'the best policy'. But it's very hard to view things clearly and objectively when your passions are aroused and everything the other person said is ringing in your ears. In times of conflict, we must be aware of two dangers.

Self-righteousness

When we assume, 'I'm innocent and he's guilty', we drift into a smug self-righteousness which has a blinding effect on us. The church in Laodicea thought they were doing fine. Jesus knew their true state:

> You say, 'I am rich; I have acquired wealth and do not need a thing.' But you do not realise that you are wretched, pitiful, poor, blind and naked (Rev. 3:17).

Part of Jesus' counsel to this church was to buy 'salve to put on your eyes, so you can see.' If we want to resolve a conflict, we must accept that we are almost definitely partly to blame for it. Like David, we must pray:

> Search me, O God, and know my heart ... See if there is any offensive way in me (Ps. 139:23,24).

When we pray like this, we should drop all self-righteousness and be prepared for God to mention what's on His list. If others were around when the incident happened, we can also ask them for an honest assessment of the situation.

Self-condemnation

The other temptation after a disagreement is to slip into hopelessness and self-pity, 'I'm useless! I always do this! What's the use anyway?' This response may seem humble, but is just as selfish as self-righteousness! We must not lose sight of God's promise:

> If we confess our sins, he is faithful and just and will forgive us our sins and purify us from all unrighteousness (1 John 1:9).

It's possible to hold onto our pride and condemn ourselves for what we've done. God wants us to stop setting ourselves a higher standard of righteousness than His. We need to admit that we've been wrong, state specifically where we've sinned, receive God's complete forgiveness and forgive ourselves.

FORGIVE

Once we've put things right with God, we must settle issues with the person with whom we've disagreed. The key to this is forgiveness — which is the 'currency of the Kingdom'. Like money, it has to keep circulating, otherwise everything gets clogged up.

Forgive freely

Jesus said:

> If [your brother] sins against you seven times in a day, and seven times comes back to you and says, 'I repent,' forgive him (Luke 17:4).

This sounds too easy for the brother. He seems to get away scot free! But our preoccupation mustn't be with what happens to him.

We must focus on forgiving the offender and releasing him from any debt that he owes us. We must even surrender our 'right' to an apology.

Forgive permanently

> Read Isaiah 43:25 and note how God deals with our transgressions.

People often say that they can forgive an offence but not forget it; God chooses to do both. As His children, we must imitate Him. Forgiveness is a decision of the will and we must stand by that decision — particularly when we have another disagreement and are tempted to rake up an old issue that has already been resolved.

Amy Carmichael was a pioneer Irish missionary to South India who established an orphage in Dohnavur which rescued children from being sold into lives of shame as slaves in Hindu temples. She understood the need to forgive in this way, and said:

> If I say, 'Yes I forgive but I cannot forget', as though the God, who twice a day washes all the sands on all the shores of all the world could not wash such memories from my mind, then I know nothing of Calvary love.

Forgive everything

Jesus said:

> And when you stand praying, if you hold anything against anyone, forgive him, so that your Father in heaven may forgive you your sins (Mark 11:25).

Clearly Jesus wanted us to forgive everyone everything. Do you feel any of the following symptoms when a certain person's name is mentioned or when you happen to see them coming towards you?

Anger rising up within you.
A tightening of the stomach.
A desire for revenge — I'll show him!
A difficulty looking him in the eye.
A strong desire to avoid him altogether.
A sense of disgust.
A need to make a critical comment about him.

If you're affected in any of these ways, you could be harbouring unforgiveness towards someone. If this is the case, you mustn't wait for them to seek your forgiveness, you forgive them freely 'when you stand praying.' When Jesus was dying on the cross, He did just this (Luke 23:34), and He left us an example to follow.

Forgive to receive

While we're on this planet, we need God's ongoing forgiveness, but we often forget that we have to do something to qualify for it.

> Read Matthew 6:12–15, and note the condition for receiving God's forgiveness.

Spend a few minutes asking God to show you any person who has wronged you, and whom you have not totally forgiven.

If people come to mind, forgive them completely, just as God has forgiven you.

Pray that God will bless them and use them powerfully for His glory.

BE RECONCILED

Just as people are reconciled to God when He forgives them their sins, so also friends will be reconciled when they forgive each other. Jesus says that if someone is holding something against us (rightly or wrongly), we must take the initiative and be reconciled to him before we pray (Matt. 5:23,24). Here are a few tips on how to do this:

Don't wait for time to heal — it won't.
Concentrate on what you did wrong, not on the other person's faults.
Confess clearly and specifically.
Use the words 'I was wrong ...' rather than 'I'm sorry'.
Beware of dealing with issues superficially. Be willing to dig into reactions and feelings so that everything is dealt with.
Ask your 'brother' to forgive you.

If the offended person is not around, you may be unable to meet him and be reconciled. Paul and Barnabas were probably in this sort of situation. It's possible that they wrote to each other and sought forgiveness. You could do the same.

> Romans 12:18 gives two qualifications for living at peace with all men. What are they?

If we've done all we can to be reconciled but our friend refuses to forgive us, we must still forgive him. In these circumstances, we must also pray about the situation and leave it with the Lord. We must also be willing to respond if He wants us to take action at a later date.

MAKE AMENDS

If we are really repentant, we will want to make amends. As soon as Zacchaeus received salvation from Jesus, he wanted to put things right:

> if I have cheated anybody out of anything, I will pay back four times the amount (Luke 19:8).

We must repay in kind. If we've somehow robbed someone of cash, we must pay back cash. If we've gossiped about someone, we must restore his reputation by seeking forgiveness from those we gossiped to and those we gossiped about.

Paul and Barnabas evidently resolved their disagreement. In 1 Corinthians 9:6, Paul refers to himself and Barnabas without any ill will. And in 2 Timothy 4:11 he expresses obvious affection for Mark who had been the cause of all their problems. All situations are redeemable — however sharp the disagreement.

Recall a sharp disagreement that you've had with someone. Review the way you tackled it and consider how you would have handled things if you'd done this study before you disagreed. Is there anything you can still do now?

Chapter Fourteen

LASTING FRIENDSHIPS

In this last chapter, we will look at a special quality which is able to make friendships last. It was rare in Solomon's time, and it's not too common today either. Solomon wrote:

> Many a man claims to have unfailing love, but a faithful man who can find? (Prov. 20:6)

This is a sad commentary on mankind. We may say all the right things, but will we have the faithfulness to see them through? Will it last? Can I be a faithful friend?

It's good to know that God is faithful. While everything around us changes, He remains totally rock-like and reliable. In the New Testament, the same Greek work is translated 'faith' and 'faithfulness', depending on the context. This is a good reminder to us that genuine faithfulness grows out of our faith in God. He wants us to be as faithful as He is.

WE'RE FAITHFUL TO OUR WORD

Proverbs 20:6 reveals the gap between what a man says and how he actually lives. We are 'faithful' if we keep our word.

R.C. Sproul has commented,

> Christians ... are required to be models of the truth. Our word should be sacred and we need to cultivate a scrupulous concern for our word. Here is where the depth of true spirituality reveals itself. A spiritual person is one whose

> word you can trust. The Christian has integrity and keeps promises. In so doing, the person bears witness to the truthfulness of the God being worshipped and served.[1]

WE SAY WHAT WE MEAN

Jesus said:

> Simply let your 'Yes' be 'Yes', and your 'No', 'No' anything beyond this comes from the evil one (Matt. 5:37).

We need to take great care when we speak, because faithfulness hinges on our saying what we mean. If we are absolutely honest, people will increasingly know that they can trust us. Then we won't need to say things like 'I promise' or 'You know you can rely on me'.

Think of some occasions when you have had some difficulty trying to convince a person that you could be trusted. Describe the context and make a note of some of the phrases you used.

WE DO WHAT WE SAY

Here are a few statements which we all make at some time or other. On the left hand side score yourself from 0–10 (0 = totally unreliable; 10 = totally reliable) to show how reliable you are in keeping your word.

___	I'll be there at 9 o'clock.	___
___	I'll post that letter on my way home.	___
___	I'll tell him that you're looking for him.	___
___	I'll return that book on Wednesday.	___
___	I'll tell him you phoned as soon as he comes in.	___
___	I'll definitely visit you.	___

___ I'll be back in ten minutes. ___
___ I'll make sure he gets the message. ___

Cover the left hand column and ask a friend to indicate in the right hand column how he rates you.

Christians are often very poor at keeping their word. One reason for this is that they don't realise that they've made a commitment. If I give some letters to a friend to post, he'll say, 'Sure, I'll post them' but he hasn't consciously added the job to his mental list of things to do. That's why some of my letters sit in people's pockets for days or weeks waiting to be posted. Here are some tips on how we can become more faithful:

Recognise that you've made a promise.
Make a note of it if you cannot do it immediately.
Carry out your promise at the first available opportunity.
Seek forgiveness for any commitment you didn't honour completely and on time.

When the disciples went out and preached the good news, we're told that:

> the Lord worked with them and confirmed his word by the signs that accompanied it (Mark. 16:20).

God always backs up His word with action. We should do the same.

We're Faithful with Things

At the end of the parable of the shrewd manager, Jesus highlights three areas in which we need to be trustworthy and makes promises to those who are faithful (Luke 16:10–12).

LITTLE THINGS

Jesus said:

> Whoever can be trusted with very little can also be trusted with much (Luke 16:10).

Hudson Taylor, the famous missionary to China, wisely commented,

> A little thing is a little thing. Faithfulness in a little thing is a great thing.

Consider some areas (not yet mentioned) where you struggle to be faithful.

HANDLING MONEY

Jesus said:

> if you have not been trustworthy in handling worldly wealth, who will trust you with true riches? (Luke 16:11)

The way we handle money determines how much of the true riches we will receive. I assume the true riches are spiritual blessings, growth in godliness, and increasing fruitfulness for God. How well do you handle your finances?

> Read Romans 13:8.

A godly leader once commented to me, 'I have learned from experience never to appoint a man with debts to church leadership.' He had discovered that unreliability with money is actually a character weakness. Here are a few tips on handling money:

Don't rob God by failing to tithe to Him.
Pay all bills on time and in full.

Repay any borrowed money as fast as you can.
Pay your taxes honestly and promptly (Rom. 13:7).
Borrow only if this is absolutely necessary and if you know you can afford to repay it. Covetousness (Col. 3.5) is idolatry, so beware of always wanting something new or different.
If money has been given to you for a purpose, make sure you use it for that purpose alone.
If you've been given money to get things for somebody else, give bills wherever possible and provide a detailed account.

ANOTHER'S POSSESSIONS

Jesus said:

> And if you have not been trustworthy with someone else's property, who will give you property of your own? (Luke 16:12)

Our attitude to borrowed items demonstrates our faithfulness as friends. A wrong attitude can put a severe strain on even an excellent friendship. If we borrow something, we should return it as soon as possible and in the best possible condition — even better than when we borrowed it. This includes anything from books and cassettes to tools, vehicles or homes.

When we read that the early Christians had 'everything in common' (Acts 2:44), we tend to overlook the responsibility attached to borrowing. Let me give you a few suggestions about this.

Don't borrow without permission.
Return a borrowed vehicle with more petrol in it than when you took it.
If you spill coffee over a borrowed book, buy a replacement and give it to the lender. (You can keep the coffee-stained one!)

Return any battery-powered item with fresh batteries in it.
If something gets damaged while you're using it, try to repair it. Don't hope that the lender won't notice. Tell him honestly and quickly what happened and what you've tried to do to rectify things. If you can't repair it, give him the money for the work to be done.
Make sure you return any borrowed item clean and properly packed.
Return any items that you've borrowed and have had for too long.

Remember, if you're faithful with things that belong to others, you will receive property of your own.

WE'RE FAITHFUL AS FRIENDS

We demonstrate our faithfulness and reliability in our words and in the way we handle things. But the real test is with people. The Lord is looking for those who will stick by their friends. All we've looked at so far is of limited value if it cannot be converted into lasting friendships. David and Jonathan give us a remarkable example of committed, enduring friendship. We read:

> Jonathan became one in spirit with David, and he loved him as himself (1 Sam. 18:1).

Loyal friendships are characterised by deep concern for the other person, not just for yourself. This means that you are as alert and sensitive to his needs and interests as you are to your own.

> And Jonathan made a covenant with David because he loved him as himself (1 Sam. 18:3).

This was a love commitment in which Jonathan promised to remain loyal to David for ever. Many people would shy away from this level of friendship, but I believe that we need to be far more willing to commit ourselves whole-heartedly to our friends. And it would help if we could express that commitment with words like, 'I love you'.

Jonathan spoke well of David to Saul (1 Sam. 19:4).

As soon as Jonathan learned of his father's murderous intentions towards David, he spoke up for his friend. A faithful friend will not only praise that friend in his absence but will also counter any gossip, slander or loose talk against him.

Jonathan said to David, 'Whatever you want me to do, I'll do for you' (1 Sam. 20: 4).

Here Jonathan demonstrated his faithfulness for David by being totally available and ready to serve in whatever way David required.

Saul hurled his spear at [Jonathan] to kill him (1 Sam. 20:33).

Jonathan loved David so much that he was willing to 'lay down his life for his friend'.

Jonathan went to David at Horesh and helped him to find strength in God (1 Sam. 23:16).

Jonathan was truly a great friend because he helped David to draw close to God. Our friendships are rooted in God and should always strengthen our walk with Him.

We read:

> there is a friend who sticks closer than a brother (Prov. 18:24).

Jonathan's relationship with David shows that this depth of friendship is really possible. The world longs to know where it can find satisfying relationships. God is relying on us to demonstrate them. But at the end of the day, it all comes down to the individual Christian. To what extent are you willing to work at deepening your friendships with others? That's a question only you can answer.

---

[1] *One Holy Passion* by R.C. Sproul © Thomas Nelson Publishers, Nashville, TN 37214.

For your notes

For your notes